Every Minister Needs a Lover

Every Minister Needs a Lover

Paul and Sybil Eppinger

BAKER BOOK HOUSE
Grand Rapids, Michigan 49516

Several people and firms graciously allowed the use of their material:

Excerpts from *The Intimate Marriage* by Howard J. Clinebell and Charlotte Clinebell. Copyright © 1970 by Howard J. Clinebell, Jr. and Charlotte H. Clinebell. Reprinted by permission of Harper & Row, Publishers, Inc.

Excerpts from *Feeling Free* by Archibald D. Hart, copyright © 1979 by Archibald D. Hart. Published by Fleming H. Revell Company. Used by permission.

Excerpts from *Loving Styles: A Guide for Increasing Intimacy* by Martin F. Rosenman (Englewood Cliffs, NJ: Prentice-Hall, 1979). Used by permission.

Excerpt from *One-to-One: Understanding Personal Relationships* by Theodore Isaac Rubin. Copyright © 1983 by El-Ted Rubin, Inc. Reprinted by permission of Viking Penguin Inc.

Excerpt from *Friends, Partners, and Lovers* by Warren Lane Molton (Valley Forge, PA: Judson Press, 1979). Used by permission of Judson Press.

Excerpt from *Open Marriage* by Nena O'Neill and George O'Neill. Copyright © 1972 by Nena O'Neill and George O'Neill. Reprinted with permission of the publisher, M. Evans and Co., Inc., New York.

Excerpt from *Marriage Is for Loving* © 1979 by Muriel James. Reprinted by permission of Addison-Wesley Publishing Co., Inc., Reading, MA.

Excerpt from *The Mirages of Marriage* by William J. Lederer and Don D. Jackson (New York: W. W. Norton & Co., Inc., 1968). Used by permission.

Excerpt from *Sex, If I Didn't Laugh, I'd Cry* by Jesse K. Lair. Copyright © 1979 by Jesse K. Lair. Reprinted by permission of Doubleday & Co., Inc.

Excerpt from *The Christian Response to the Sexual Revolution* by David R. Mace (Nashville, TN: Abingdon Press, 1970). Used by permission.

Excerpts from *Active Loving* by Ari Kiev (New York: Thomas Y. Crowell, 1979). Used by permission.

Excerpt from *The Edge of Adventure* by Keith Miller and Bruce Larson, copyright © 1974 . Used by permission of Word Books, Publisher, Waco, TX 76796.

Excerpt from *Living, Loving & Learning* by Leo F. Buscaglia (New York: Ballantine Books, Random House, 1982). Used by permission.

Excerpt from *Straight Talk to Men and Their Wives* by James C. Dobson, copyright © 1980. Used by permission of Word Books, Publisher, Waco, TX 76796.

Excerpt from *No Fault Marriage* by Marcia Lasswell and Norman M. Lobsenz. Copyright © 1976 by Marcia Lasswell and Norman M. Lobsenz. Reprinted by permission of Doubleday & Co.

Excerpts from *The Person Reborn* by Paul Tournier, translated by Edward Hudson. Copyright © 1966 by Paul Tournier. Reprinted by permission of Harper & Row, Publishers, Inc.

Excerpt from *Personhood: The Art of Being Fully Human* by Leo Buscaglia (New York: Random House, 1978). Used by permission.

Excerpt from March 1976 *Unity Magazine,* quoted by J. Sig Paulsen.

"What Every Child Needs," reprinted with permission from the National Mental Health Association, 1021 Prince Street, Alexandria, VA 22314-2971.

Excerpt from *Happiness Is Still Homemade* by Cecil T. Myers, copyright © 1969. Used by permission of Word Books, Publisher, Waco, TX 76796.

Excerpt from *Creative Divorce* by Mel Krantzler (New York: M. Evans and Co., Inc., 1974). Used by permission.

Excerpts from *Success Is a Moving Target* by Robert A. Raines, copyright © 1975. Used by permission of Word Books, Publisher, Waco, TX 76796.

Excerpt from *Christians Doing Financial Planning: A Handbook for Individuals and Families.* © 1976 by Commission on Stewardship, National Council of Churches. Used with permission.

Excerpt from "Anatomy of an Illness (As Perceived by the Patient)" by Norman Cousins, *Saturday Review,* 5/28/77. Reprinted by permission.

Contents

Preface

PAUL:

> She came out of the shadows—
> beautiful, alluring, seductive.
> I had been married just a short time,
> and I loved my wife,
> but, there she was—
> calling me,
> tempting me,
> challenging me,
> exciting me.
> Taking my time;
> exciting my interests,
> teasing my fantasies,
> fulfilling my desires.
> Sometimes she was slow and quiet,
> sometimes fiery and tempestuous,
> but always attractive,
> always alluring,
> and, slowly, I realized
> my marriage was in danger.

By that time, we had been married for twelve years, and now I was giving Sybil so little of my time, so little of my interest, so little of my energy. It was not intentional, but now I realize that everything had been given to that beautiful seductress: *the church.*

SYBIL:

Those first twelve years with Paul were frustrating ones for me. I had entered marriage starry-eyed, very much in love, and determined that our marriage was going to be different. I would be the perfect wife and ours would be the perfect relationship! I had truly attempted to mold and shape my own life and that of our children to Paul's welfare and the church's demands. But those demands were limitless, or so it seemed, and since I was unable to meet them completely, I found myself feeling inadequate and defeated. I continually tried harder and put more and more pressure on myself to be at every meeting at church and be involved in all its activities, to teach Sunday school, to be supportive of Paul, to be a creative and involved mother for our four daughters. I felt eaten alive. There were such diverse obligations, and I considered myself a failure because I was unable to meet them. I also felt less and less important to my husband because he was so involved everywhere else that there was little time or energy left for me. Each of us had little to give to the other. When we realized our marriage was in jeopardy, we reluctantly went to see a marriage counselor. We were embarrassed, hesitant, frightened. We were *pastor and wife!* People were supposed to come to the pastor; he was supposed to have all the answers.

But we went. For about eight months we worked with our counselor to rediscover our own selves and each other. We revealed secrets, expressed anger, forgave sins, and reclaimed our love in the process.

PAUL:

During this time I had been involved in a doctoral program and was searching for a theme for my dissertation. One question began to gnaw at me: "Is any other pastor facing this situation in his marriage? Am I alone?" We ministers go to our meetings, conventions, and conferences and play a "Little Jack Horner" game. We put in our bureaucratic thumb, pull out a statistical plum, and declare, "What a good person am I." We tell about our largest church attendance, most successful offerings, most exciting programs; but we seldom share our hurts, pains, temptations, embarrassments, failures—especially as they pertain to us personally or maritally. People in other careers do the same thing. They share their successes, but rarely share themselves.

As I wondered whether I was the only minister going through a marriage crisis, I decided to write a thesis on the topic. I entitled it, "The Success and Failure of Marriage Among American Baptist Pastors." For my research, I sent questionnaires to five hundred clergy and their spouses and interviewed a number of divorced clergy and their ex-spouses. Out of that research, I discovered the following basic causes for marital failures among the clergy:

1. Functionalism instead of personal intimacy
2. The inability to share deep feelings
3. Limited communication

4. The "fishbowl" existence of the ministry
5. The pressure of time demands
6. Confusion concerning the role of the spouse
7. Divorce not being seen as an option
8. Sexual problems
9. Salary limitations
10. Failure on the part of seminaries and churches to be strong support systems

The results of this research have been validated by our own experience in marriage. We have observed these trouble spots as we have counseled other ministers and their spouses. These ten factors continue to appear to be the prime pressures on marriages among the clergy.

Our idea is quite simple. Instead of the church being the "seductress," *ministers are married to the church.* If that is true, each of us needs to make our spouse our lover—"Every Minister Needs a Lover." We need to give our marital partner our attention—sneak the time, send the gifts, share in-depth communication, explore exciting new sexual practices—do all those things a person does for a lover. But, in this case, the lover is the spouse.

This book is designed to give ministers and their spouses, and other couples as well, thirty days to look, think, talk, and grow in their marriages, because every minister *does* need a lover. It is jointly written from a personal standpoint as a male clergy person and a female marriage-and-family therapist. (We celebrate and support the growing number of women entering the ministry. Where the minister is female, please make the necessary gender changes to accommodate your situation.)

Acknowledgments

The writing of this book has made us aware of our debt to many people who have accepted, loved, and supported us and our family through these years of marriage and ministry. The members of the churches we have pastored, our family members, and our friends have played a significant part in our lives, and we are deeply grateful for what they have meant to us.

To Keith Miller, who read the manuscript and gave us thoughtful feedback, and to those persons who read the manuscript and tested it in their own marriages, we say thanks. Glenn and Kathy Harman, Gary and Jane Zook, Jack and Glenda Hinton, Phil Towle, and Bev Leuenberger shared insights that helped us to finalize our efforts. To Mary Rogers and Kathi Pernell, who typed the manuscript many times, we say thank you.

To our four daughters—Damaris, Priscilla, Stephanie, and Monica —who have made life beautiful and meaningful for us, we say thanks for making us family.

Introduction

How to Use This Book

This work/play book is designed to be a thirty-day experimental program of guided marriage enrichment for couples to make their marriages richer, fuller, more meaningful, and more exciting than before. You are the focal persons of the book—the only ones who can make your marriage an exciting and enriching adventure. This book is an effort to help you focus on the various aspects of your marriage that often suffer stress because of your profession or your spouse's.

We urge you to allot a period of uninterrupted time each day to be spent with each other. Then let this book be a guide for your marital growth.

First, each day, we will invite you into our lives. As openly and honestly as possible, we will share our joy, pain, hurt, healing. Because our own marriage enrichment is not yet completed, we are sharing ourselves with you where we are now, even though many of these episodes come out of our past experience. The initial portion in each chapter will come from our own lives.

Second, we will suggest a section of Scripture to form a foundation stone for your discussion. This will be without our theological comment or interpretation, allowing the Holy Spirit to make the Word relevant to your life, background, tradition, and experience. Space has been allowed for you to jot down your own personal notes on the biblical truths presented.

Third, we will share a paragraph from another resource that we feel has special bearing on the subject of the day. These excerpts have been chosen with care from persons who have shown great insight into the many facets of marriage, but if you have access to other material on that topic that has greater meaning to you, please read it as well. The important thing is that thoughtful words be allowed to stretch and enrich your mind and heart at this juncture of your life. Here, too, you may wish to add some personal comments.

Fourth, all of these parts of each day's experience are preparatory for the most important time: the discussion by the two of you about your marriage and how you can most dynamically enrich it. To help in that experience, we have posed several questions for you to discuss every day after you have each made some notes on your own. Each partner should answer the questions on a separate piece of paper. For that process, we suggest the following guidelines:

1. *Let each person express his or her feelings about that topic in your marriage.* The basic feelings recognized by many authorities are those of anger, fear, sorrow, joy, and love. (To make a feeling statement is to say, "I feel sad," or "I feel glad," or "I feel angry," and so on.)

2. *This is the time to listen to each other.* It is not the time to judge, condemn, debate, or seek to persuade the other person to your point of view.

3. *Establish a time, place, and setting that will provide uninterrupted conversation.* Since body language is an important part of communication, position yourselves comfortably, facing each other. The aim is to facilitate the give-and-take of the listening process.

4. *Do everything you can to use "I" statements in your discussion.* This is the opportunity for you to share yourself seriously, openly, and honestly by declaring, "This is what I think . . ." or "This is how I feel. . . ."

5. *Before you end the session, seek to resolve any conflict that may arise.* If a potentially serious issue becomes apparent, seek out a qualified counselor to assist you in resolving that issue.

6. *If you choose to discuss only one of the suggested questions, please do so.* But keep the others to discuss at a later time. We hope you will want to come back to these questions many times.

For each day's session, we have composed a brief closing prayer to focus on the topic at hand. We urge you to let that simply be a catalyst for you to complete each day's sharing experience with your own prayers.

Let this entire work/play book be your personal journal. Especially as you read the Scripture and supplemental material, write your own thoughts, responses, feelings, and prayers, so that this book becomes truly yours. Remember, the focal point of these insights is to help your marriage become more alive in a ministerial setting—to allow your spouse to become your lover.

1

Functional—But Not Intimate

"I don't know what you're going to say . . .
but I sure hope you listen to it!"

PAUL:

We were in a heated exchange. We had been married long enough to know the exact words and tone of voice to use and the precise timing to attack the other's emotional jugular vein, but also to know that we could fight without its being the end of our marriage.

It was the Saturday before Valentine's Day, and Sybil knew that every year on the Sunday before Valentine's Day I preach a sermon on love and Christian marriage. After the sermon, the couples in the congregation are invited to come to the front of the sanctuary and repeat their wedding vows to each other. It has always been a touching, important service and a sermon to which I give special attention. But now, within hours of that service, we were burying each other in verbal and emotional garbage. We had reached an impasse, with both of us feeling unheard, uncared for, unresponded to—a complete lack of intimacy. Sybil broke the deadlock with "I don't know what you're going to say in that sermon tomorrow morning, but I sure hope you listen to it!"

That got to the focal point of our fight and told me that one of the most damaging factors in any relationship is that though we learn how to "function" superbly, far too seldom do we ever learn what real intimacy is all about. We clergy learn how to do our jobs in a professional way—attending committee meetings, composing sermons, conducting church business, visiting the sick, doing denominational work, and being involved in the endless tasks of a minister. Our spouses also have their

15

specific tasks to do, and often we operate very well as a couple in managing our homes, working in our churches, participating in social and community events. But we can become so involved in and so deeply committed to these functional aspects of marriage that we never really open ourselves to each other. As a result we don't allow ourselves to take risks and become vulnerable to each other. We don't become "one flesh," one total unit. For any marriage to be genuinely fulfilling, intimacy—the creative, growing experience that unites two people emotionally, mentally, psychologically, spiritually, and physically—must be the vital, central core.

Scripture

The LORD God said, "It is not good for the man to be alone. I will make a helper suitable for him."

So the LORD God caused the man to fall into a deep sleep; and while he was sleeping, he took one of the man's ribs and closed up the place with flesh. Then the LORD God made a woman from the rib he had taken out of the man, and he brought her to the man.

The man said, "This is now bone of my bones and flesh of my flesh; she shall be called 'woman,' for she was taken out of man."

For this reason a man will leave his father and mother and be united to his wife, and they will become one flesh.

The man and his wife were both naked, and they felt no shame.

Genesis 2:18, 21–25

Personal Notes

Further Insight

In that most intimate of friendships called marriage, the opportunities and demands for a relationship of depth are pervasive. Intimacy is an art with as many expressions as there are artists to express it. It is often expressed in the sharing of thoughts and ideas and

Comments

feelings. It is expressed in shared joys and sorrows, in respect for the deepest needs of the other person, and in the struggle to understand him. Intimacy does not suggest a saccharine sentimentalism; it can be expressed in constructive conflict which is the growing edge of a relationship. Intimacy is not a constant, but is expressed in varying degrees in the ebb and flow of day-in, day-out living. An intimacy is never a once-and-for-all achievement but must be nurtured throughout marriage; with this care, it grows and changes with the stages and seasons of marriage.

From Clinebell and Clinebell,
The Intimate Marriage, pp. 24–25.

Questions to Discuss

(to be answered on a separate piece of paper by each partner)

1. For me, a most intimate time with you was . . .

2. If we were to become more intimate with each other in practical ways, I think it would . . .

3. From my understanding of the Clinebells' description of intimacy (above), two ways I am willing to seek deeper intimacy in our relationship are . . .

Our Prayer

O God, who became intimate with us in Jesus, help us to become intimate with each other in marriage. . . .

Amen.

2

Sharing True Feelings

"Emotionally, I was a chameleon."

SYBIL:

Throughout my lifetime the most difficult feeling for me to deal with has been that of rejection. Early in our marriage I learned that Paul expressed his anger by becoming silent, distant, polite, noncommunicative. The distance between us felt like abandonment and rejection, and this resulted in near panic for me. Without consciously realizing it, I began to adapt my behavior, attempting to predict what would please or displease Paul and choosing my actions on that basis. Emotionally I was a chameleon, adapting my "color" to my surroundings. Using this camouflage for protection, I attempted to display only what was safe for me. Instead of sharing with Paul my feelings of aloneness and insecurity, I made every effort to produce a setting lacking in conflict so I could avoid Paul's displeasure.

This meant an even further denial of my feelings. For example, I wanted more of his time and attention. I wanted a portion of the energy, enthusiasm, and dynamism I saw him exuding in his work and his relationships there. What I got was an exhausted husband who fell asleep a half hour after arriving home from his ever-present evening meetings. I felt angry, ignored, taken for granted—but I kept silent about my emotions. I also felt as if I were being unreasonable and unwilling to make sacrifices for God's work. I was trapped by my conflicting emotions and thoughts, believing I was less than a committed Christian for having them and inadequate to resolve them.

What mixed messages I must have given Paul—such intense feelings inside me and such cooperative behavior being displayed on the outside!

19

My lack of genuineness and integrity cost us something in our relationship. What we were missing was true intimacy, which is possible only when individuals can be real—open and vulnerable—with each other.

Scripture

You, however, did not come to know Christ that way. Surely you heard of him and were taught in him in accordance with the truth that is in Jesus. You were taught, with regard to your former way of life, to put off your old self, which is being corrupted by its deceitful desires; to be made new in the attitude of your minds; and to put on the new self, created to be like God in true righteousness and holiness.

Therefore each of you must put off falsehood and speak truthfully to his neighbor, for we are all members of one body. "In your anger do not sin": Do not let the sun go down while you are still angry, and do not give the devil a foothold.

Ephesians 4:20–22

Personal Notes

Further Insight

It has been my experience that this is the most common mistake that Christians make regarding their emotions. They teach themselves very skillfully how to deny them. This is, of course, true also of people in general in our culture. From our earliest years we are taught that it is bad to be "emotional," and that feelings must, at all costs, never be shown. If it only stopped there, it would not be so bad, but we take it further, and in order for us not to show our feelings we train ourselves in not acknowledging them even to ourselves.

Let me illustrate this point by asking you to conduct a little experiment.

Comments

The next time you are with someone, stop the conversation and ask him to describe to you how he is feeling at that instant. You will be surprised at how difficult it is for that person to describe accurately what he is feeling. I know, because as psychotherapists we try to get people to do this many times each day. Better still, stop yourself periodically and see whether you can describe to yourself how you are feeling. It will be just as difficult. Why? We have trained ourselves in the art of denial and the avoidance of feeling. We simply don't want to face our real inner selves where our feelings reside.

The problem can become further aggravated when you become a Christian. You move into a community of believers who, generally speaking, tend to resist the expression of real feelings. Partly this is because we are afraid of true intimacy; partly it's because this is how we perpetuate our own denial of feelings; and mainly it's because we fear being seen as a failure. "What will they think?" is the most neurosis-producing thought I know, and this idea—coupled with an unhealthy attitude toward any form of failure, especially within the Christian community—leads us to be very protective of our feelings and to avoid giving any acknowledgment to them.

From Hart, *Feeling Free*, p. 19.

Questions to Discuss

1. The feelings that I share most easily with you are . . .

2. Feelings that I have swallowed in the past that might still be impacting me in regard to our relationship are . . .

3. When I share my deepest feelings with you, I feel [threatened, excited, vulnerable, and so on] . . .

Our Prayer

O God, we realize that Jesus experienced and shared the deep feelings of anger, sorrow, and love in his life. Help us to be honest with *our* feelings and share them, so that we might bring constructive vitality to each other. . . .

Amen.

3

Tuning In to the Message

"Daddy, I'm sorry I hit you,
but you make me so mad . . ."

PAUL:

Our four daughters were young, and two of them were in a terrible fight. Angry words were exploding from their bedroom. Finally, one stalked into the bathroom and slammed the door behind her. Being a "savior type," as father, Christian, and pastor, I felt it was my job to go in and help her calm down.

But another factor was present. That daughter's middle name is "Joy," and from the day she was born, there was that special excitement that did bring me deep joy whenever I was around her. The outward effect on me is that I simply want to laugh with delight when I am in her presence. I was experiencing that feeling as I followed her into the bathroom that day and sat down on the bathtub. She was seething with anger, and her feelings had been hurt—her little fists were clenched, her eyes almost literally shooting sparks—and yet that is when this inner joy hit me again. I began to chuckle. She looked at me for a second and then, quicker than I could respond, hit me as hard as she could with a right and a left just under my chin. I was shocked and didn't know what to do. First of all, it really hurt; second, according to my tradition, children did not treat their parents that way. In that one moment, my daughter had transferred her anger from her sister to me, and we stood eye-to-eye, staring at each other. Finally, after about thirty seconds, she broke the silence and in a quiet little voice said, "Daddy, I'm sorry I hit you," and then the volume of her voice rose and she almost screamed, "but you make me so mad when you laugh at me!" All at once I realized that for six years I had not been receptive to her feelings. So I began to talk: "Honey, I'm sorry. You probably can't understand this, but there is something about you that just gives me a continuous sense of joy and happiness. But now I realize that my laughter has communicated to you that I haven't really heard you, that I haven't been sensitive to your feelings and your needs. I want to ask your forgiveness for that."

We stayed in the bathroom for thirty minutes and talked, and that half-hour session of sharing and receiving each other's feelings transformed our relationship, which is still being blessed from that encounter, fifteen years later.

The same principle holds true in marriage relationships. We need to stay receptive to each other's feelings without worrying what society, the church, our parents, or anyone else will think. Only then will there be a freedom to share with each other whatever feeling we might be having at a given moment.

| **Scripture** | **Personal Notes** |

Jesus entered the temple area and drove out all who were buying and selling there. He overturned the tables of the money changers and the benches of those selling doves. "It is written," he said to them, "'My house will be called a house of prayer,' but you are making it a 'den of robbers.'"

The blind and the lame came to him at the temple, and he healed them. But when the chief priests and the teachers of the law saw the wonderful things he did and the children shouting in the temple area, "Hosanna to the Son of David," they were indignant.

"Do you hear what these children are saying?" they asked him.

"Yes," replied Jesus, "have you never read, 'From the lips of children and infants you have ordained praise'?"

And he left them and went out of the city to Bethany, where he spent the night.

Matthew 21:12–17

Further Insight

We human beings are extremely complex emotional organisms. The extent of our emotions (and the way in which we cope with them) is probably what separates us most widely from the rest of creation. Animals cannot feel as we do. Their responses are conditioned responses more than they are the expression of free, emoting creatures. Your dog may wag its tail as a sign of love to you, but the love you are capable of showing to others, as well as to the dog, far surpasses anything your pet has to offer. Your feelings do not have to be conditioned responses to what others have done for you, but have the capacity to be totally unconditional.

Through your emotions, you have the potential for deriving the greatest pleasure and joy which life has to offer. They provide the excitement and thrill of living that no other aspect of your being can provide. Take away your capacity to feel (as is done in certain forms of brain surgery) and life suddenly loses its luster. No longer can you feel the thrill of excitement, the flush of embarrassment, the sobering of a down feeling, and the happiness and joy of some new experience. Your feelings, both pleasant and unpleasant, give your life sparkle and should therefore be embraced, understood, and taken charge of in such a way that they are used to enhance your life.

On the other hand, your emotions have the ability to cause you the greatest misery that it is possible for a human being to suffer. Lose control of an unpleasant emotion such as depression and you will soon lose any reason

Comments

for wanting to stay alive. This should not cause you to want to avoid your emotions, but rather motivate you to turn them to your good. God has given you the capacity for utilizing your complex emotional system for your benefit, and it should be a force that draws you nearer to Him and not, as it so often becomes, a means of self-destruction.

From Hart, *Feeling Free*.

Questions to Discuss

1. You help me release my feelings of [e.g., anger, sorrow, fear, joy, love, or sexuality] when you . . .

2. I think I help you express your feelings most authentically when I . . .

3. The way I would most like to express my feelings to you is by . . .

Our Prayer

O God, nobody ever had to guess whether Jesus was angry or not—he told them. Nobody ever had to guess whether Jesus was sorrowful or not—he wept. Nobody ever had to guess whether Jesus loved or not—he died! Help us always to express our feelings directly and honestly to each other. . . .

Amen.

4

Self-Image and Self-Esteem

Leaners, Loners, Losers, Lovers

SYBIL:

Paul was preaching a sermon about "relating" in the context of marriage and had asked me to join him in dramatizing the various styles in which people relate. One was the "leaners," and to illustrate we stood face to face about four feet apart and leaned into each other with our arms on each other's shoulders. This is a dependency style, and we talked about the destructiveness inherent in that kind of relating. Another style is used by "loners," and for that we walked away from each other with our backs turned and began to talk about the way we were feeling at that very moment. Here a sense of loneliness, isolation, and lack of contact was the dominant element in the feeling experience. We suggested that this extremely independent style, too, can contribute to the collapse of a relationship.

The next style we planned to illustrate called for one person to place a foot on the back of the kneeling partner, thus indicating dominance and passivity, the latter being the "loser" position. Since we wanted all of these dramatizations to be as spontaneous as possible, we had not planned who would do what in each vignette. In this style, Paul had apparently planned to kneel, indicating that I was the dominant person in our relationship. Since that possibility never entered my mind, I immediately dropped to the floor and looked up imploringly at Paul. The women in the congregation broke into spontaneous applause, not because they supported that stance, but rather to affirm that many of them felt dominated in their marriages. Paul was caught off guard—speechless for a minute—then gestured with his arms extended in a rather helpless, uncertain fashion and mumbled, "She beat me to it!"

He recovered his composure, rediscovered his power of speech, and we came to the style that is most creative and constructive: "lovers." To illustrate this, we both stood on our own two feet, without leaning on each other at all. At the same time, we held hands, symbolizing that we are connected in a relationship in which we can come face-to-face to talk, hug, share, make love, or pray. However, because we are not imprisoned by each other, we can move out and away to form friendships and work or share various activities with people away from our relationship as a couple.

Obviously, the "lover" style of relating has the strongest, most creative effect when each partner brings a healthy self-image into the marriage. Self-image (the way you perceive yourself) and self-esteem (the way you feel about that perception) result from a process that begins at birth. These concepts develop through an individual's interpretation of the reactions of significant people—parents, relatives, teachers, close friends, and religious advisors. They are continually impacted by input from other people and our realization that we have succeeded or failed in living up to our own standards and goals. But the essence of self-image and self-esteem is each person's own responsibility. When each of us accepts that responsibility for ourselves, we can choose to share openly with our partner, give love and support when needed, and create the "lover" lifestyle of healthy interdependence.

Scripture   ## Personal Notes

Hearing that Jesus had silenced the Sadducees, the Pharisees got together. One of them, an expert in the law, tested him with this question. "Teacher, which is the greatest commandment in the Law?" Jesus replied: "'Love the Lord your God with all your heart and with all your soul and with all your mind.' This is the first and greatest commandment. And the second is like it: 'Love your neighbor as yourself.' All the Law and the Prophets hang on these two commandments."

Matthew 22:34–40

Further Insight

Self-acceptance provides a firm foundation for building love. All too often, relationships fail because one or both of the partners believes that he or she is not worthy of being loved. Although an intimate relationship can contribute to self-acceptance and self-esteem, a feeling that one is worthy of love is usually a prerequisite. The situation is analogous to that of the individual who states, "I wouldn't join any club that has low enough standards to invite me to join." Feelings of unworthiness and unlovableness often defeat a relationship before it begins. Without self-acceptance, happiness will be elusive. Happiness comes from within, and the belief that another person can make us happy is an illusion. "We tell ourselves," writes Ken Keyes, "if only I could find the right person to love, then I would be happy. So we search for someone who our addictions tells us is the right person—and we experience some pleasurable moments. But since we don't know how to love, the relationship gradually deteriorates. Then we decide we didn't have the right person after all! As we grow into higher consciousness, we discover that it is more important to be the right person than to find the right person.

Being the right person involves knowing yourself. Socrates' simple admonition "Know thyself" provides a path for achieving the good life, but it is more difficult than it sounds. To know yourself fully, you have to face yourself honestly, looking through facades, shams, and pretenses. You have to reconcile discrepancies between saying

Comments

and doing and discrepancies between accomplishments and hopes. You have to accept a simple psychological truth: You create, rather than find, yourself."

From Rosenman, *Loving Styles,* pp. 32–33.

Questions to Discuss

1. On a scale of one to ten (*one* being the lowest and *ten* the highest), this is how I evaluate my self-image when I'm at my job:

   0   1   2   3   4   5   6   7   8   9   10

   On a scale of one to ten, this is how I evaluate my self-image when I'm with you:

   0   1   2   3   4   5   6   7   8   9   10

2. The following are five positive qualities *about me* that I celebrate when I'm with you:

3. The following are five positive qualities *about you* that I celebrate when I'm with you:

Our Prayer

O God, you declared that we were to love ourselves. So help me now to love every life-giving aspect of my life, realizing that it all comes from you. . . .

Amen.

5

Trust Is a Partnership Matter

"Hey, look at me! I'm counting on you!"

PAUL:

It was a worship service for which we had planned for weeks, one that was going to be taped for television and shown on Christmas Eve. Thousands of people would be watching this service at one of the most important times of the year. All of the choirs in the church would sing, our handbell choirs would ring, and everyone else would be pulling out all the stops to make it the finest possible declaration of the good news of Christmas.

The choirs had rehearsed and timed their music so that we knew exactly how long they would require during the one-hour service. We had calculated the Scripture readings and other portions of the service, too. Everything had come down to the fine point of exact timing that was imperative for the telecast schedule. I knew I would have twenty-one minutes and thirty seconds for the sermon. I prepared it in great detail, knowing almost to the second how much time each point of the sermon would take and where I needed to be in the sermon as the minutes were counted off.

Sybil and I decided that she would be the timekeeper for the sermon. She would sit in the first row and signal to me when I had twenty minutes left for the sermon, then fifteen minutes, ten minutes, and five—our—three—two—one. Even though we had hosted a television program dealing with family issues every week for five years, this worship service was a special event. On the Sunday morning of the taping there was a buzz of excitement throughout the congregation. The cameras were ready; the lights were on; the TV crew members were in their places.

33

Then the service began. The music was superb, with every choir seemingly outdoing itself. The Scripture reading came through clearly and distinctly, and then it was time for the sermon. I began to preach and looked down at Sybil, who gave me the twenty-minute signal. I progressed into the sermon, knowing that at a certain point I should have fifteen minutes left. I looked at Sybil, but there was no signal, so I looked a little closer. What was happening? She was no longer "with me." Was she sleeping? A sense of panic gripped me, and I wanted to yell, "Hey, look at me! I'm counting on you!" I continued with the sermon, feeling disconcerted and hoping she would "come back" and let me know the time still available for the sermon.

SYBIL:

When Paul began preaching, I quickly calculated the times at which I should give my signals: 11:40—twenty minutes, 11:45—fifteen minutes, 11:50—ten minutes, and so on. After I had given the twenty-minute signal, I settled back in the pew with a small digital clock in my hand on my lap. As I listened to the sermon I marveled at Paul's ability to capture and hold the attention of his audience. I glanced at my clock—11:43—two minutes more until the next signal.

My mind wandered for a moment to the open house we were having that afternoon. Had I completed all the necessary arrangements? Did I have enough people scheduled to help? I glanced back at my clock—11:47. How could that be? Then it dawned on me. I must have misread 11:45 as 11:43! Now there were thirteen minutes left and I hadn't signaled Paul for the fifteen! I belatedly gave the signal but he wasn't even looking at me. Two more minutes passed and he glanced at me. Then it was almost time for the ten-minute signal! I flashed it, glad he was looking my way. But how could he adjust the message to fit the remaining minutes?

PAUL:

My silent prayer was answered. Sybil looked up, smiled, looked back at her watch—but now panic gripped her face! Very quickly she gave me a signal that there were only ten minutes left for me to conclude the last two-thirds of the sermon. Even while I continued preaching, various thoughts raced through my head, and feelings about this break in trust reverberated through my consciousness. Primary was that I could adjust, compensate, and rectify the sermon by myself. The other was that we are a team, and I trust the shared commitment we have to our partnership and our work.

Later I reflected that to wander mentally during the sermon was relatively insignificant, for it signaled merely a lapse in the *functioning* of our relationship. However, a break of trust in the *intimacy* of a relationship is a tremendously important danger signal. Self-trust comes first and then you will be able to trust your partner.

Scripture

In that day this song will be
    sung in the land of Judah:
We have a strong city;
    God makes salvation
    its walls and ramparts.
Open the gates
    that the righteous nation may
    enter,
    the nation that keeps faith.
You will keep in perfect peace
    him whose mind is steadfast,
    because he trusts in you.
Trust in the LORD forever,
    for the LORD, the LORD, is
    the Rock eternal.
                Isaiah 26:1–4

Personal Notes

Further Insight

Trust precludes self-doubt, a feeling of unlovability, poor self-esteem, strong feelings of vulnerability, and paranoia. Trust first depends on one's relationship with oneself, and *then* on one's relationship with the participating partner. Real self-love and real self-acceptance determine the potential for trust. Self-trust predisposes us to trust others. But the same self-trust and perceptive ability protect us from compulsive trust of those who realistically demonstrate that trust in them would be trust destructively misplaced.

Trust implies a high degree of mutual comfort and a low degree of self-defense tension. It means you have confidence in your partner not to hurt

Comments

or manipulate you. You feel confident
that your partner will support your
efforts at self-realization. Such support and confidence are a function of
concerned feeling for each other and
are not related to fair or foul weather,
moods of any kind, favors done or not
done, or any external happening. . . .

High esteem, hope, and compas-
sion for self—and the relating process
in its infinite complexity—and for the
relationship in question is basic to
trust.

From Rubin, *One-to-One*, pp. 106–7.

Questions to Discuss

1. I think I trust myself
   (a) on the job, when I . . .
   (b) in our marriage, when I . . .
   (c) in my own personal growth, when I . . .

2. Three times when I have felt you trusted me were:

3. I wish you would trust me more about . . .

Our Prayer

O God, who trusted us enough to send your only Son to us, help us to be trusting and trustworthy to our own personhood, to each other, and to you. . . .

Amen.

6

Mutual Support Systems

A Jar of Affirmation

PAUL and SYBIL:

We had just arrived home from a trip to the Middle East, and the church was having a special fellowship for us, not just to welcome us home but also to celebrate the beginning of our third year of ministry with this congregation. We sang and shared, and people stood to speak and express words of affirmation that were very meaningful. But then, from underneath the pulpit, one of the leaders brought a large, wide-mouthed jar with a fancy ribbon on the top and invited all those present to write on a 3 x 5 piece of paper a word of thanks or encouragement, addressed to us. The leaders gave approximately five minutes for that exercise and then collected the papers and put them in the jar. We were to open that jar every morning and take out one note to read. As we write this, we've been doing that for over three and a half months. Every day we know there is going to be a special word of encouragement and affirmation. It's an amazing feeling to begin each morning with a strong word of support and love from a member of the congregation. They could not have given us a better gift.

Here are a few examples:

"You have a terrific vision for the church and its future. Hang in there!"

"I appreciate your optimism for this church."

"Whatever you want to do, go for it."

"When you're feeling discouraged at events outside of your control, remember to lean heavily upon our Lord. *He* is our *strength!*"

"May God especially bless you and yours on the day you draw this note."

"I appreciate your tremendous vitality."

"If you ever feel deserted, that you're left alone, remember Elijah—he had 7,000 times the support he thought he had!"

"Hang in there when the going seems slow and people don't seem to be responding. You're building for the future."

"I appreciate your having the courage to act on your convictions."

"Thank you for your extreme sensitivity to others."

"The angels stoop down in wonder to see what God is working out in your lives."

"I appreciate the love and concern you have for each one in your congregation."

"Thank you both for the way you affirm people while challenging us to grow."

Since that fellowship evening, we've wondered why we don't do that with each other in marriage. If we were to give words of affirmation to each other every day, we could lift each other up and strengthen each other's self-image as well as our marriage. Inherent in that process is our being able to hear and accept the affirmation offered. Such a gift is similar to the gift of God's grace in that it must be accepted to be meaningful.

Scripture

The men were sent off and went down to Antioch, where they gathered the church together and delivered the letter. The people read it and were glad for its encouraging message. Judas and Silas, who themselves were prophets, said much to encourage and strengthen the brothers. After spending some time there, they were sent off by the brothers with the blessing of peace to return to those who had sent them. But Paul and Barnabas remained in Antioch, where they and many others taught and preached the word of the Lord.

Acts 15:30–35

Personal Notes

Further Insight

Mutual respect in partnership is not rooted in role, function, or sex. It is not determined by societal assignments for husband and wife, or notions about man's work and woman's work, or the stereotypes of "men are that way," or "that's just like a woman." It has to do with the ability to have a unique appreciation for the partner as a person with his or her personal gifts and needs. When our partner sees us uniquely, we feel esteemed and respected. It is this balanced, mutual respect that enables equality in the marriage. If I see my partner as inferior, I will not treat her as an equal. I will not adequately respect her. While unequals may be partners in certain enterprises, a healthy marriage demands equality.

Our best research today indicates that perhaps more than ever before young people are tending to marry peers. Now, if we can enable them to escape the stereotypes of role, function, and sex which tend to support notions of inequality, perhaps men and women can begin to treat each other fairly and reciprocally. There are some marvelous differences between men and women, but there is nothing that dictates feelings of inequality of persons, so that either is exploited or abused.

From Molton,
Friends, Partners, and Lovers, pp. 82–83.

Comments

Questions to Discuss

1. I feel affirmed in our communication when . . . because . . .

2. I feel affirmed in our sex life when . . . because . . .

3. One way I would like more freedom to be me in our relationship is . . .

Our Prayer

O God, help us to be so interdependently related to you that we might give freedom to each other, choosing to serve as a mutual support system in all we do. . . .

Amen.

7

The Sending Process in Communication

"Adding some 'fine print' worked wonders!"

PAUL:

Sybil and I met in a summer missionary-orientation program in Nashville, Tennessee. She was from a Methodist church in Mississippi and I was from an American Baptist church in Colorado. We had both graduated from college and had committed ourselves to three years of missionary work in an overseas field.

Our meeting was almost one of those proverbial love-at-first-sight experiences. I had not realized that one of the stipulations of our missionary contracts, which we had already signed, was that we could not marry for the three years of our service. I was devastated. All that summer we thought, talked, and prayed about whether we should break our contracts and get married, or fulfill our signed commitments and trust that our love would last through a three-year engagement period. We decided to gamble on the latter. After six weeks of being together, getting to know each other, and sharing hopes and dreams, we parted. During the three years we were engaged, we saw each other only three times.

Early on, we had confronted the issue of how to keep a relationship alive for three years. How do you share each other's hurts and pains? How do you let the other person know that this is who you are, this is the way you are growing and changing, this is what your future hopes are, what your dreams encompass, what you desire? The only way is by communication, and for us that had to be through letters. We soon discovered that there are only so many ways you can say, "I miss you and love you" and "I wish we were married," in a letter. After we had covered that we began sharing in a deeper way who we were, what our lives were becom-

42

ing, what our faith was all about. We shared doubts, hurts, pain, failures, and our dreams for the two of us together. Adding some 'fine print' worked wonders!

We sent scores of letters to each other. One of the most important learning experiences of our relationship was discovering that for a relationship to stay alive and growing, messages must continually be sent to each other. A creative sending process involves "I" statements, such as "I feel," "I think," "I desire," "I fear," "I believe." When the communication is oral rather than written, it also requires allowing your body language, the tone of your voice, and your actual words to be congruous so that you are sending one clear message. The sending process is the first important step in communication.

Scripture

"Ask and it will be given to you; seek and you will find; knock and the door will be opened to you. For everyone who asks receives; he who seeks finds; and to him who knocks, the door will be opened.

"Which of you, if his son asks for bread, will give him a stone? Or if he asks for a fish, will give him a snake? If you, then, though you are evil, know how to give good gifts to your children, how much more will your Father in heaven give good gifts to those who ask him! In everything, do to others what you would have them do to you, for this sums up the Law and the Prophets."

Matthew 7:7–12

Further Insight

All the discoveries that we make through communicating with ourselves—our thoughts, beliefs and concepts of self—are only ideas until we crystallize them and give them meaning and substance in words. Thus we come to know ourselves even better through disclosing ourselves to others. "Full disclosure of the self to at least

Personal Notes

Comments

one other significant human being," writes Dr. Sidney Jourard in *The Transparent Self,* "appears to be one means by which a person discovers not only the breadth and depth of his needs and feelings, but also the nature of his own self-affirmed values." Revealing ourselves openly and honestly to others is the most important means of knowing the self.

Furthermore it is one of the most important means by which our mates come to know us. "Through my self-disclosure," writes Jourard, "I let others know my soul. They can know it, really know it, only as I make it known." True intimacy between mates, and mutual growth, is based on the ability to open up and share your inner selves without fear of judgment—not only your likes, but your dislikes, your doubts as well as your hopes. We become authentic beings to each other by "taking the first step at dropping pretense, defenses, and duplicity."

From O'Neill and O'Neill,
Open Marriage, pp. 112-13.

Questions to Discuss

1. I find I can most easily send messages to you when . . .

2. I find it most difficult to send messages to you when . . .

3. I believe I can improve the sending process to you in our communication by . . .

Our Prayer

O God, your message of love to us was sent so clearly in Jesus. Help us to be straightforward, honest, and direct in our communication with each other. . . .

Amen.

8

Receiving the Communication

"Men ought always to pray, and not to think!*"*

SYBIL:

A young woman in our congregation was going through an intensely stressful time. Vivacious, attractive, and sensual, she had become involved in a relationship that was tearing her apart. For months she had been able to handle it, but then the doubts and guilt began to build. She was hospitalized for several weeks and given medication to help her calm down. Finally, she was released from the hospital and was back in church the next Sunday.

That morning Paul preached a sermon on prayer based on a parable of Jesus illustrating that "men ought always to pray, and not to faint" (Luke 18:1 KJV). He had carefully designed the sermon as an attempt to inspire people to pray, declaring that prayer is the force and the strength that empowers us, vitalizing our lives so that we do not cave in. Built into the sermon was the repeated phrase, "Men ought always to pray, and not to faint." When the service was over, this woman left the sanctuary through the door where Paul and I were greeting people. She clasped our hands and told us that she had been uplifted by the service; that she was now transformed. "I am a new person because of that one sermon," she said. "I will never forget Jesus' message: 'Men ought always to pray, and not to *think!* Now I can stop worrying about everything. I'll just pray and let God work it all out!"

We didn't correct her wording. We didn't suggest any changes but, rather, allowed the Spirit to minister to her need.

As Paul and I talked later, we agreed that each person listening to a sermon hears it through a personal filter system in the light (or darkness)

46

of his or her own needs. We each hear what is spoken to us through the interpretation of our own experiences.

We realized that this also happens in one-to-one relationships. I only hear what I am conditioned to hear. If I am exhausted, my sense of hearing is distorted. If I feel distant, what I hear is muffled. If I am guilty of being disloyal in some way, I am defensive and receive blurred information.

An important aspect of communication is receiving the message clearly. Not only should we pay attention to the way we speak and the way we send a message, but also to the way we listen and perceive what the other person is saying. Reception can be refined and enhanced by not assuming automatically that I understand my partner's meaning but by asking questions to clarify that meaning and trusting the explanation that is given.

Scripture

In them is fulfilled the prophecy of Isaiah:

"'You will be ever hearing but never understanding; you will be ever seeing but never perceiving. For this people's heart has become calloused; they hardly hear with their ears, and they have closed their eyes. Otherwise they might see with their eyes, hear with their ears, understand with their hearts and turn, and I would heal them.'

"But blessed are your eyes because they see, and your ears because they hear. For I tell you the truth, many prophets and righteous men longed to see what you see but did not see it, and to hear what you hear but did not hear it.

"Listen then . . ."

Matthew 13:14–18

Personal Notes

Further Insight

Emotional intimacy is openness and closeness at the feeling level rather than the thinking level. Couples who have developed emotional intimacy

Comments

can transact in many ways—they laugh together, take care of each other, feel safe to say what they want to say.

One of the best ways to expand emotional intimacy is to improve communication between partners. If both think more about listening to than being listened to, their communication improves dramatically. Emotional intimacy grows when two people take time to listen to each other, to care about the other's feelings, and to guard their relationship. Sometimes this means setting aside time to discuss problems at work or at home, to discover how a partner is coping on a day-to-day basis. More often it is just remembering to say, "I hear you."

When people are listened to, they feel accepted. Because they feel accepted, they feel freer to be their true selves and are less rejecting of others. Because they are less rejecting and see "the best" in others, they help partners become liberated and enjoy doing it.

From James, *Marriage Is for Loving,* p. 136.

Questions to Discuss

1. I feel listened to when you . . .

2. You can help me know you hear me by . . .

3. I can improve my listening to you by . . .

Our Prayer

O God, help us to listen to you and to each other. May every aspect of our beings be open to the messages that are all around us. . . .

Amen.

9

Responding to the Message

"Now we know you're human, and we love you!"

PAUL:

We were in the middle of our marital crisis and had finally gone to a counselor, which was the first major hurdle for me to overcome. I had been a pastor for twelve years. *I* was the one who was supposed to have all the answers. I had read many books and had counseled other people. From my particular Christian background, if one was walking the Christian life, Jesus would handle every hurt, every pain, every temptation. "Christ is the answer!" and "victorious Christian living" were the slogans and heartbeats of my very being. But somehow, in terms of our marriage, there was no answer from Christ and no victory for me. So, finally, I had acquiesced and we had gone to a counselor.

Now the second major hurdle confronted me. How do I tell my congregation that I, the person who is supposed to have all the answers, am going to a marriage counselor? Although I was embarrassed, ashamed, and frightened, I took the advice of my counselor and began to contact the officers of the church to tell them not only that Sybil and I were in counseling, but also some of the details that had fractured our marriage. I knew that any one of them could have damaged my professional life severely, but I also knew that I had to share with them what was happening in my life. Their response was absolutely unbelievable. They accepted us, loved us, and encouraged us in our counseling process. Several weeks later, almost as an aside in a Sunday-morning sermon, I said that I knew some in the congregation were experiencing difficulties with personal or family problems, and I wanted them to know that I recognized what they were confronting because Sybil and I were in marriage counseling at that time. Again, the congregation responded with unanimous openness, support, warmth, and love. They hugged Sybil and me, promised their prayers, and affirmed in different ways that "Now we know you're human, and we love you!" Wow! Almost immediately my ministry entered a new dimension. Because people now saw me as a real person, some called to minister to me, and others to ask for help. Self-disclosure may not always work out that way, but it certainly did for me.

The response they gave to my message is a key to all communication. Not only does a person *send* a message and a listener *receive* that message, but a response is always involved when true communication is taking place. Letting the speaker know that the message is heard, whether that be with a word or an action response, is imperative. In marital situations, communication that involves sending, receiving, *and* responding is essential for maintaining a creative, vital, growing, and intimate relationship.

Scripture

"I tell you the truth: Among those born of women there has not risen anyone greater than John the Baptist; yet he who is least in the kingdom of heaven is greater than he. From the days of John the Baptist until now, the kingdom of heaven has been forcefully advancing, and forceful men lay hold of it. For all the Prophets and the Law prophesied until John. And if you are willing to accept it, he is the Elijah who was to come. He who has ears, let him hear.

"To what can I compare this generation? They are like children sitting in the marketplaces and calling out to others:

"'We played the flute for you, and you did not dance; we sang a dirge, and you did not mourn.'"

Matthew 11:11–17

Personal Notes

Further Insight

In the Pacific there are a large number of tropical fish called tangs. These beautiful multi-colored crea-

Comments

tures are noted for a spot of intense color near the dorsolateral fin. In certain of the tangs, this spot conceals a poison spur, and in others, a sharp spur which is used for defensive protection. Finally, there are the tangs with the brightest, most luminescent and striking dorsolateral spots of all, and these tangs have no stinger whatsoever. Yet, even so, other fish give them wide berth.

The message received by the fish is that they should beware of the tang's bright-colored spot. The fact that some tangs don't really have a defensive spur cannot be known by the other fish until they actually test the expectation by encountering the tangs in combat. Since they avoid such explicit encounters, they never learn which tangs have the stinger. The story has a moral for married couples: Don't condemn it until you've tried it!

Analysis of slow-motion films of couples in various situations reveals that the two individuals continually "speak" to each other by non-verbal methods (gestures, actions, facial expressions, and the like). When people have been married for a period of time—even a few weeks or months—they develop a mutually understood labeling system. Certain gestures are assumed to indicate specific moods or emotions. This process of classification is natural, but it has a serious flaw. It ignores equifinality, which means that a particular end result may arise from one of several different beginnings; thus, if a wife rubs her nose whenever she is getting angry at her husband, he will soon recognize the connection. But suppose she also rubs her nose when it itches? His immediate defensive behavior (when

he believes she is angry) may set off
in the wife a spark of annoyance that
then convinces him that indeed she
was angry. Old patterns, unlike sol-
diers, don't die or fade away. They
remain, unless clarified by the wisdom
and experiences of the spouses.

From Lederer and Jackson,
The Mirages of Marriage, pp. 102–3.

Questions to Discuss

1. Ways I think I have responded positively to you in the past are . . .

2. Times I have appreciated your response to my communication are . . .

3. Ways you can respond more clearly to me are . . .

Our Prayer

O God, help us respond appropriately to each other, showing that all messages are heard. May that response be clear, understandable, and personal. . . .

Amen.

10

Sexuality and Affection

"We could hardly wait to be alone!"

PAUL and SYBIL:

The car was sitting in front of the church, jammed with every wedding gift, every piece of clothing, every material item that either of us owned. As we pulled away from the curb, people were still throwing rice, still calling out their good-byes and congratulations to us. It was our wedding day.

We had met three years earlier in a missionary-orientation program. Sybil was then on her way to the Republic of the Philippines for three years under the auspices of the Methodist Church, and Paul was to serve with the American Baptist churches in Japan. For those three years we were separated most of the time, seeing each other only three times. During those three visits, we had to be careful and very limited in the physical expression of our love because those cultures did not approve of two unmarried people touching. We are both very physical people, so limiting our touching and overt expression of affection was an extremely difficult part of our courtship. Somehow we had managed to control ourselves.

Now the day had arrived! The ceremony was finished—we were husband and wife! No longer were physical restraints necessary. As we drove out of town, moving away from our wedding into the two weeks of our honeymoon, we began to express our love with touching, laughter, and erotic behavior. We could hardly wait to be alone!

Through the years has come our deepening conviction that sex, open affection, and physical touching are imperative for the joy and success of any marriage. Hugs, holding hands, arms around each other's waists as we stand together, an active sex life—all have become an integral part of our relationship.

Physical touching is important with people in general, but especially with those to whom we are committed. To learn to ask for affection, and to respond to it in like manner, is essential for an exciting, intimate relationship.

Scripture

Now one of the Pharisees invited Jesus to have dinner with him, so he went to the Pharisee's house and reclined at the table. When a woman who had lived a sinful life in that town learned that Jesus was eating at the Pharisee's house, she brought an alabaster jar of perfume, and as she stood behind him at his feet weeping, she began to wet his feet with her tears. Then she wiped them with her hair, kissed them and poured perfume on them.

When the Pharisee who had invited him saw this, he said to himself, "If this man were a prophet, he would know who is touching him and what kind of woman she is—that she is a sinner."

Jesus answered him, "Simon, I have something to tell you."

"Tell me, teacher," he said.

"Two men owed money to a certain moneylender. One owed him five hundred denarii, and the other fifty. Neither of them had the money to pay him back, so he canceled the debts of both. Now which of them will love him more?"

Simon replied, "I suppose the one who had the bigger debt canceled."

"You have judged correctly," Jesus said.

Then he turned toward the woman and said to Simon, "Do you see this woman? I came into your house. You did not give me any water for my feet,

Personal Notes

but she wet my feet with her tears and wiped them with her hair. You did not give me a kiss, but this woman, from the time I entered, has not stopped kissing my feet. You did not put oil on my head, but she has poured perfume on my feet. Therefore, I tell you, her many sins have been forgiven—for she loved much. But he who has been forgiven little loves little."

Luke 7:36–47

Further Insight

What we needed as babies was more loving, which to a baby primarily means more touching. We aren't babies any more, so we can give and receive love through other means than physical touching. But I find that physical touching is tremendously valuable to us as a gauge of how able we are to reach out and love. We need the touching for itself. But we are so good at lying to ourselves about our ability to love that only touching can keep us honest. Touching is visible. We can see if we're doing it or not, and we can see the effects of the touching. . . .

Now, I understand that physical touching is just a part of meeting our adult needs for human contact. Symbolic touching, emotional openness and closeness to the other is probably the way we'll meet our needs most of the time. But touching helps us here, too, because we can kid ourselves we're really being close but if we find we can't reach out and physically touch the other person in some way, we probably aren't as close as we thought we were.

From Lair, *Sex,*
If I Didn't Laugh, I'd Cry, pp. 57–60.

Comments

Questions to Discuss

1. I like to be touched . . .
   I like to touch . . .

2. I don't like to be touched . . .
   I don't like to touch . . .

3. For me, a touch is . . .

Our Prayer

O God, just as Jesus touched and was touched—physically, emotionally, and spiritually—help us to touch each other with meaning, joy, and intimacy. . . .

Amen.

11

Celebrating Our Sexuality

"When I was born again . . .
I became a tigress in bed!"

PAUL:

I have never heard the biblical view of marital sex so dramatically verbalized than by a woman who came into my study to talk about becoming a part of our church fellowship. She was in her early thirties and had been married for about twelve years. I already knew that she had had a strong conversion experience three or four years before moving to our city. When I asked her about that experience, she began to spell out the changes that had come into her life. She very matter-of-factly said, "I became a different wife to my husband." I asked her to explain what she meant, and she replied, "I mean physically."

Immediately my mind began to rerun old tapes that were a part of my background. The church I was raised in was a very conservative one, and we had been taught that God was somewhere "up there" and that he was spiritual, pure, holy, and good. We were "down here" and unholy, impure, sinful, and sexual. Because of those contrasts, God and sex simply did not belong together. Even to think about God and sexuality, let alone put them in the same sentence, was an almost "unforgivable" sin. Although I had moved out of that mind-set, these old tapes began running through my mind. My fear, therefore, was that this woman meant that she had been sensuous, affectionate, and sexual before her conversion, but that when she became a Christian someone had told her that sex was bad even within marriage—and that God and sex did not mix.

When I began saying something like that to the woman, she interrupted: "No, Paul, it was just the opposite. When I was born again, I was

59

born again sexually, too, and therefore I became a tigress in bed! My husband could not believe he was married to the same woman."

Somehow that personifies the biblical wholeness of sexual attitudes needed between married partners. Sexual activity becomes a means for expressing our acceptance of each other: a thanksgiving for our sexuality, an excitement about sharing our lives physically, and a desire to bring each other total physical satisfaction. That is beautifully expressed in the creation story, where (in Gen. 1:27) the word that we translate as *male* is "pointer" (obviously the penis), and the world *female* is actually "opening" (obviously the vagina). So the creation story really declares that God created us with the amazing gift of sexuality—and we know that he "saw all that he had made, and it was very good" (v. 31a). Therefore, sexuality and sexual sharing in a marriage is meant to be exciting and erotic, which is perhaps the most Bible-based and Christian attitude we can have toward spousal intimacy.

Scripture

The most beautiful of songs, by Solomon.

The Woman

Your lips cover me with kisses; your love is better than wine.

There is a fragrance about you; the sound of your name recalls it. No woman could keep from loving you.

Take me away with you, and we'll run away; be my king and take me to your room. We will be happy together, drink deep, and lose ourselves in love. No wonder all women love you!. . .

The Man . . .

You, my love, excite men as a mare excites the stallions of Pharaoh's chariots.

Your hair is beautiful upon your cheeks and falls along your neck like jewels.

But we will make for you a chain of gold with ornaments of silver. . . .

How beautiful you are, my love; how your eyes shine with love!

Song of Songs 1:1–4, 9–11, 15 (TEV)

Personal Notes

Further Insight

Out of my own experience as a marriage counselor, I had occasion to ask a wife, during one of my interviews with her, about her sex relationship with her husband. She replied that they had no problems in this area. Such an assurance cannot always be taken at face value. In this case, however, the wife went on to add a word of explanation, to the effect that before they had intercourse, her husband always said a prayer. This is such an unusual situation that I asked the wife if she would care to tell me more about it, because I was very much interested. She replied that there was really very little to tell, except that this had been their custom throughout their married life. I asked what sort of prayer her husband offered. She smiled, and said it was always the same prayer, and a very familiar one. As they lay together in bed, in a loving state of anticipation, he simply said, on behalf of them both, "For what we are about to receive, may the Lord make us truly thankful."

It has often seemed to me that this married couple might be regarded in a symbolic way as taking us to the heart of the Christian response to the Sexual Revolution. In their simple, artless fashion they were making the fundamental affirmation that sums up the Christian doctrine of human sexuality; a doctrine that is clearly enough stated in the Bible, but which has been lost for a long time in our bewildering complexity of theological confusion. It is to our shame that it has taken a sustained onslaught from the secular world to awaken us to the distortion of the basic Christian truth that has so

62

long obscured what the Church should have been saying to men and women about the way in which God made them.

What these two people were saying was precisely what the early Hebrews said, and what the early Christians said until the somber philosophies of the Orient and of Hellenism clouded the sky. But because Christians stopped saying it, the Church fell into a long era of error and darkness, from which it is only now at last slowly emerging.

And so our prayer is for the progressive enlightenment of the Church. Only when it can say, sincerely and without equivocation, "Thank God for sex," can it begin to respond in any authentic manner to the challenge of the Sexual Revolution.

From Mace, *The Christian Response to the Sexual Revolution*, pp. 132–34.

Questions to Discuss

1. For me, sex,
   a. when I was growing up, was . . .
   b. early in our marriage, was . . .

2. Today, things that occur during the day that affect me sexually are . . .

3. The attitudes about sexuality I'd like to change in our relationship are . . .

Our Prayer

O God, help us to have the same kind of joy and openness toward each other as the lovers had in the Song of Songs in your Word. . . .

Amen.

12

Sharing the Joy of Sex

". . . a marvelous time of lovemaking"

SYBIL:

We sat around the dinner table on a Monday evening several years ago, sharing an experience that has regularly enriched our lives as a family. Every evening we ask the question, "What was the most important thing that happened to you today?" and allow time for each person around the table to respond. That little ritual allows all of us to speak about whatever we wish, for as long as we want and without being interrupted, and then for the rest of the family to celebrate or lament with the speaker.

Monday is the "Sabbath" at our house. Paul and I both take that day off. Often, when the children were younger, we would get them off to school and then go back to bed for a time of lovemaking. That had been our wonderful experience on that particular Monday.

As we went around the dinner table that night, sharing our most important events, it finally came Paul's turn to speak. He said, "Oh, I got a lot of yard work done today." I responded by turning to him with a quizzical, flirtatious, "Oh?"—thinking that he would add something like, "Your Mom and I enjoyed being together today." He surprised both the children and me by responding, "Okay, girls, the most important thing for me today was that your mother and I had a marvelous time of lovemaking." Instantly there was laughter but also some uncertainty. Then the boldest of our children began asking her own questions, "When? Where?" and so on.

Somehow, we need that same childlike openness with our partners, asking questions about what each other likes or dislikes, and daring to share our own likes, dislikes, and sexual fantasies. That also includes daring to be experimental and adventuresome so that our sex life continues to grow and be a source of joy, excitement, and fulfillment.

Scripture	**Personal Notes**

The Man
How beautiful you are, my love!
How your eyes shine with love
    behind your veil.
Your hair dances like a flock
    of goats
bounding down the hills of
    Gilead.
Your teeth are as white as
    sheep that have just been
    shorn and
    washed.
Not one of them is missing;
they are all perfectly
    matched.
Your lips are like a scarlet
    ribbon;
how lovely they are when you
    speak.
Your cheeks glow behind your
    veil. . . .
The look in your eyes, my
    sweetheart and bride,
and the necklace you are
    wearing
have stolen my heart.
Your love delights me,
    my sweetheart and bride.
Your love is better than wine;
your perfume more fragrant
    than any spice.
The taste of honey is on your
    lips, my darling;
your tongue is milk and
    honey for me.
Your clothing has all the
    fragrance of Lebanon.

My sweetheart, my bride, is a
    secret garden,

a walled garden, a private
    spring;
there the plants flourish.
They grow like an orchard of
    pomegranate trees
and bear the finest fruits.

The Woman
Wake up, North Wind.
South Wind, blow on my
    garden;
fill the air with fragrance.
Let my lover come to his
    garden
and eat the best of its fruits.
    Song of Songs 4:1–3, 9–13, 16
                    (TEV)

Further Insight

Lack of sexual responsiveness often
reflects a failure to understand the way
you and your loved ones relate to each
other. Sexual problems, indeed, reflect
many unidentified feelings and expectations. Inadequate sexual responses
may communicate both conscious and
unconscious motivations: fear of commitment, inability to assume responsibility for sexual acts, self-denial, mar-
tyrdom or a desire to control.

You may, at times, experience diffi-
culty in accepting sexual feelings. The
fusion of sexual and affectionate feelings, in particular, often creates conflicts of people in their closest relationships. Or you may, as many people
do, focus on the orgasm as the primary
goal of sexual contact. You will achieve
more satisfaction when you focus on
the immediate sensations being experienced, allowing the natural rhythms of
the body to bring you to a state of
relaxation, rather than thinking of what
is supposed to happen. Passive attitudes prevail where compliance and

Comments

concern for acceptance, rather than genuine involvement, predominate. Failure to experience orgasm may, ironically, result from a preoccupation with it, for preoccupation with performance and orgasm diminishes your capacity to lose your self-consciousness and to flow with the sexual act.

If this sounds familiar, consider the following when you next experience such concerns: Do you have doubts about your capacity to love or to respond to someone who loves you? Perhaps you can readily accept loving feelings but develop anxiety about sexual ones. Try to let go of your inhibiting thoughts, allowing your body to relax and events to unfold. Let things happen. Too much conscious effort to experience total absorption in the sexual act prevents it from happening naturally.

You can learn to visualize and concentrate on the immediate sensations you experience. Allow yourself to become absorbed in them and focus on the present, not on "results." By thinking of the one you love, and not yourself, you will increase your chances of letting go and overcoming your inhibitions about becoming absorbed in the sensuality of the experience.

From Kiev, *Active Loving*, pp. 117–18.

Questions to Discuss

1. Concerning my sexual desires and needs, I want you to know . . .

2. I believe I can better respond to your sexual desires and needs by . . .

3. Something I would like us to try sexually is . . .

Our Prayer

O God, help us to communicate our marital love—to listen, hear, and feel such intimacy that we truly are "one flesh.". . . .

Amen.

13

The Growth of Sexual Intimacy

" . . . we've rediscovered what we've been missing.
Wow!"

PAUL:

I still remember the day when I was about eight years old and heard my first four-letter word. There were three or four of us boys on the school playground and, amidst a lot of giggling, shoving, and boisterousness, someone said the fateful word. I had never heard it before and obviously did not know what it meant. One of the other boys did not know its meaning either, so we both said almost at the same time that we would go home and ask our mothers. "No, no, don't do that," the more knowledgeable guys declared. "They will die!"

That was an early highlight in my sex education, and for years my sexual understanding stayed almost at that level. Sex play, fondling, caressing, and "making love" were seen as wrong and sinful, something to be hidden. Sex was something boys tried to do to show their manhood, and girls fervently resisted to show their femininity and purity.

When Sybil and I were first married, we were both highly responsive to each other's body. For the three years we had been engaged, five thousand miles of South China Sea had kept us physically separated. After we had ceremonially affirmed the sanctity of our marriage commitment, our sexuality became holy, beautiful, and fulfilling. For over twenty-five years, we have been learning how to bring more physical pleasure to each other. Sharing erotic fantasies, reading sexual books together, and experimenting with different lovemaking practices have brought us to the firm conviction that sexual activity and sexual growth can and should be an essential part of every creative marriage relationship.

Scripture

Personal Notes

The Man

What a magnificent girl you
    are!
How beautiful are your feet
    in sandals.
The curve of your thighs
    is like the work of an artist.
A bowl is there,
that never runs out of spiced
    wine.
A sheaf of wheat is there,
    surrounded by lilies.
Your breasts are like twin deer,
    like two gazelles.
Your neck is like a tower of
    ivory.
Your eyes are like the pools
    in the city of Heshbon,
near the gate of that great
    city.
Your nose is as lovely as the
    tower of Lebanon
that stands guard at
    Damascus.
Your head is held high like
    Mount Carmel.
Your braided hair shines like
    the finest satin;
its beauty could hold a king
    captive.
How pretty you are, how
    beautiful;
how complete the delights of
    your love.
You are as graceful as a palm
    tree,
and your breasts are clusters
    of dates.
I will climb the palm tree
    and pick its fruit.
To me your breasts are like
    bunches of grapes,
your breath like the fragrance
    of apples,

and your mouth like the finest
wine.

The Woman
I belong to my lover, and he
desires me.
Darling, I have kept for you
the old delights and the new.
Song of Songs 7:1–10, 13b (TEV)

Further Insight

To deepen sexual intimacy, a couple needs to enjoy sex in ways that will cause it to feed their love. A marriage is vital to the extent that there is a uniting of these two forms of intimacy—physical and psychological. Satisfaction of the personality hungers of one's mate, particularly his sexual ego needs, is extremely important. Each partner should test his behavior in the marriage in terms of how well he uses opportunities to make his mate feel more adequate, attractive, and lovable as a male or a female. To say by words and behavior, "You're terrific in bed," or "We make sweet music together," or "You made last night heavenly!" causes one to prize his or her sexuality, which makes it easier to be loving, passionate, and giving the next time. Good sex interaction not only expresses one's own feelings, but . . . the partner needs to feel valued and felt as a person of worth, as a real live human being. The wedding ceremony contains an implicit truth about relationships in the phrase, "love, honor and cherish." A man and woman cannot really love deeply unless they also honor (esteem, appreciate, respect) and cherish (nurture, prize, hold dear) each other. The total quality and value of the relationship

Comments

affects the meaning and satisfaction derived from sexual intercourse. There is a fundamental difference between alienated and intimate sex—the difference is love.

Cultivating the art of lovemaking is another way to increase sexual intimacy. Most couples, if they try, can enhance their repertory of sexual enjoyment; they can help make sex play better for themselves and each other. It takes time to improve sexual artistry, and that is often a problem in our frantic society. Setting aside time for regular "let's-enjoy-each-other" nights or days is a practice that pays big dividends. One couple near the termination of marriage counseling reported: "Up until we started having 'our nights,' sharing, including sex, got the tag ends of our time. We allowed other less important things to squeeze lovemaking into late, hurried moments which made it terribly mechanical. In the last months we've rediscovered what we've been missing. Wow!"

From Clinebell and Clinebell,
The Intimate Marriage, pp. 141–42.

Questions to Discuss

1. The things I enjoy most about our sex life are . . .

2. Ways I could help improve our sex life are . . .

3. A sexual fantasy I would like you to play out with me is . . .

Our Prayer

O God, because you made us physically as well as spiritually and psychologically, help us to enjoy each other totally in our physical life together. . . .

Amen.

14

Handling Conflicts

"Happily married people do *disagree sometimes."*

Neither of us really remembers the first fight we had after we were married, but we do remember the feeling emerging from that conflict. It was one of almost total and utter confusion.

SYBIL:

We came from such different backgrounds as far as "marital conflict" is concerned. I never saw my mother and father argue. My mother was an only child raised by her mother, who had been widowed when my mother was six years old. With no siblings and only one parent in the home, there were limited opportunities for my mother to learn to deal with conflict. My father, on the other hand, was the youngest in a family of fourteen children, eleven of whom were girls. His two brothers were already adults and away from home when he was born. Very much the focus of love and attention in his family, he also had little conflict with which to deal. When I was growing up, I rarely saw my parents disagree on anything. I'm still not certain if they avoided or denied their differences or if they handled them privately, but I did not see any real arguments. So I made the assumption that because they loved each other and were committed to each other, they didn't have any conflicts.

PAUL:

When my parents were first married, they lived on a farm in Kansas and struggled to survive. During the dust-bowl days of the thirties, they lost almost everything they had and moved to a small town to try to put their lives back together again. I don't remember my parents having difficulties with each other when I was a small boy, but as I grew older I sometimes noticed that disagreements came into their relationship. Although there were many good times, there were also some harsh words and hurt feelings expressed in front of us children. Yet I never saw them *resolve* an issue.

From these divergent experiences, Sybil and I joined together in a marriage relationship, one believing that happily married people never fight, and the other believing that there is never a chance to resolve an issue, so the best thing to do is ignore disagreements. Whenever it was that we had our first conflict, you can imagine how devastating it was for us. For Sybil the fantasy that happily married people never fight was shattered. For me there was the hopeless feeling of never being able to resolve an issue. These two alternating feelings infected our relationship until we were finally able to work them out with the help of a marriage counselor. We have learned that conflict is a natural and inevitable phenomenon, that happily married people *do* disagree sometimes. Even more important, we now realize that in conflicts there can be a resolution of issues and that the discord itself can become a time of creative growth.

Scripture

Therefore each of you must put off falsehood and speak truthfully to his neighbor, for we are all members of one body. "In your anger do not sin": Do not let the sun go down while you are still angry, and do not give the devil a foothold.

Do not let any unwholesome talk come out of your mouths, but only what is helpful for building others up according to their needs, that it may benefit those who listen. And do not grieve the Holy Spirit of God, with whom you were sealed for the day of redemption. Get rid of all bitterness, rage and anger, brawling and slander, along with every form of malice. Be kind and compassionate to one another, forgiving each other, just as in Christ God forgave you.

Ephesians 4:25–27, 29–32

Personal Notes

Further Insight

Loving is not a fixed state of mind, but an active and fluctuating inter-action between two people whose feelings are continually evolving, creating new configurations and patterns reflecting both continuity and change. How you handle similarities and differences, closeness and separation, conflicts and crises, determines how well the relationship grows. In the best relationships—those characterized by a healthy interdependency—two autonomous people derive strength from each other. In the worst relationships—characterized by excessive dependency—they drain and stifle each other.

Elements of conflict—overdependency, fear, hostility—occur in the natural evolution of all relationships, but come to dominate the unsatisfactory ones. Seeking to find strength in other people, you may become unnecessarily dependent on them, even denying your own strength in order to ensure their support. Or, you may take the opposite approach and deny any of your own weaknesses in an effort to dominate others. In either case, interpersonal conflicts are likely to develop. The bottled-up resentments which excessive dependency and/or dominating behavior are bound to produce and generate are anxiety, anger, and even hatred. When these feelings predominate, the relationship may be said to be in a state of constant conflict. It is as astonishing as it is depressing to realize how many "working marriages" fall into this category. And the situation can be avoided!

Comments

Interpersonal conflicts usually have these elements in common:

1. the failure of two people to measure up to each other's unrealistic expectations;
2. efforts to "control" or change each other (these invariably lead to an escalation rather than a reduction of conflict);
3. failure to preserve separate identities;
4. failure of each person to take steps to modify his or her own behavior in order to maximize mutual satisfaction;
5. failure to maximize the positive features of time spent together.

From Kiev, *Active Loving,* pp. 77–78.

Questions to Discuss

1. When I look at the way my parents (or parent-substitutes) handled conflicts, I realize . . .

2. If I could characterize in one word the way we handle conflict, it would be . . . [Explain.]

3. Ways we could improve the way we handle conflict in our relationship are . . .

Our Prayer

O God, we know we should deal with our conflicts and not just let them lie there to stagnate and poison us. Help us to resolve our differences lovingly and creatively. . . .

Amen.

15

Fighting Fair

"We don't have to be taught to 'talk dirty' to each other!"

PAUL and SYBIL:

It's amazing how most of us humans seem to have a built-in aptitude for dirty fighting. We live in a win/lose society. If the other team wins, mine loses. When you get the best grade on a test, I have to settle for something less. If "the girl of my dreams" chooses my rival, I lose. This syndrome of competitiveness affects all aspects of our lives and pressures us to fight unfairly to win. In marriage, almost before the minister has said the benediction at the wedding ceremony, we somehow know the exact words to speak, the tone of voice to use, and the time to use them to hurt our partner most destructively. We don't have to be taught to "talk dirty" to each other!

SYBIL:

As I mentioned in an earlier chapter, my mission in life when we married was to be the perfect pastor's wife. Unfortunately, in my own mind that meant to do and be everything Paul wanted me to be and do. First of all, I took his name. Then I officially became a member of his denomination, even though I had served as a missionary for another denomination. I tried to be at every women's meeting, every choir practice, every Bible study and prayer meeting, every reception—all in an attempt to role-play "pastor's wife" perfectly. Any time there was a difference of opinion, all Paul had to do was ask a question to remind me that I wasn't perfect, and that would paralyze me. "Have you gained a little weight lately?" "Do I have any clean shirts?" (when I hadn't done the ironing). "Hasn't this bill been paid yet?" (when I was handling the checkbook). He would say these things with a smile on his face and a softness in his voice. Then, instead of dealing with the underlying issue about which we were struggling, my attention would be drawn to the surface criticism, which would disorient me and sidetrack us both. That was dirty talking and dirty fighting! And it was intensely personal in its effect.

But now it is different. Now I know I do not have to be perfect and I am no longer devastated by such questions. In fact, such questions no longer exist. Now when we fight we have learned to try to stay with the subject; to speak for ourselves (making "I" statements); to listen to each other; and to avoid put-downs by words, tone of voice, or body language. We struggle with the issue openly until we reach a solution and also resolve our feelings about it. Fighting fair has become a creative goal in our relationship.

| Scripture | Personal Notes |

We all stumble in many ways. If anyone is never at fault in what he says, he is a perfect man, able to keep his whole body in check.

When we put bits into the mouths of horses to make them obey us, we can turn the whole animal. Or take ships as an example. Although they are so large and are driven by strong winds, they are steered by a very small rudder wherever the pilot wants to go. Likewise the tongue is a small part of the body, but it makes great boasts. Consider what a great forest is set on fire by a small spark. The tongue also is a fire, a world of evil among the parts of the body. It corrupts the whole person, sets the whole course of his life on fire, and is itself set on fire by hell.

All kinds of animals, birds, reptiles and creatures of the sea are being tamed and have been tamed by man, but no man can tame the tongue. It is a restless evil, full of deadly poison.

With the tongue we praise our Lord and Father, and with it we curse men,

who have been made in God's like-
ness. Out of the same mouth come
praise and cursing. My brothers, this
should not be. Can both fresh water
and salt water flow from the same
spring? My brothers, can a fig tree
bear olives, or a grapevine bear figs?
Neither can a salt spring produce fresh
water.

James 3:2–12

Further Insight

As with most skills, the ability to
deal effectively with conflict develops
through involvement, understanding
and practice. Applying these principles to your relationship might, to
stretch an analogy a bit, be compared
with learning to play tennis. A book
on tennis will be helpful only if you
practice the techniques outlined. Even
then, many principles will be difficult
to master. Knowing all the steps
required for an effective tennis stroke
is much easier than performing them
at the crucial moment. Often you will
be aware of your mistakes, but you
will require time for correcting them.
At some stages learning a correct
technique, perhaps a way of holding
the racket, will at first be uncomfort-
able, but will become a good habit as
it brings about more successful results.
The initial self-consciousness inherent
in following rules will gradually dis-
appear as you gain proficiency through
practice.

The principles described below are
easy to read, but their application
requires the involvement and the co-
operation of both partners. A basic
assumption is that you both are willing to work on improving your intimate relationship.

Comments

The following are the principles for effectively facing conflict:

Basic Ground Rules

1. Complain with a spirit of good will.
2. Avoid attacking each other.
3. Focus on the here and now.
4. Admit your feelings.

Specific Techniques

5. Select an appropriate time.
6. Be specific.
7. Deal with one issue at a time.
8. Ask for a reasonable change.
9. Listen carefully.
10. Try to accept and understand.

Finding a Solution

11. Think, explore, meditate.
12. Be willing to accept incomplete resolution.
13. Consider compromise.
14. Avoid trying to win.

From Rosenman, *Loving Styles*, pp. 85–86.

Questions to Discuss

1. Of the fourteen items listed above, the five I think we do well on are . . .

2. Of those fourteen items, the five I think we most need to work on are . . .

3. After we have a fight or serious disagreement, I feel . . .

Our Prayer

O God, help us in our conflicts to seek to build our relationship, not to break each other or simply try to win the argument. Be in and with us so that even our fights might be redemptive for us and life-giving to our marriage. . . .

Amen.

16

Choosing Vulnerability

"Have I let anyone else know who I really am?"

PAUL:

Sybil has always been an open person. She knows instinctively how to share with people. To the extent that she is willing to reveal so much of herself to others, she becomes vulnerable to them. For me, being open has been a difficult process because I had built up so many barriers to being vulnerable. Somewhere in my development I had learned that a Christian, especially a minister, was to be perfect. Knowing that I could never attain that, I became an expert at hiding my true self from everyone.

Reinforcing my self-concealment was the admonition given to me by some very well-meaning people over the years—that a minister should remain objective, never becoming too close to anyone and certainly never sharing anything negative, painful, or personal with others. Out of that background, I became a little island of self-sufficiency, never allowing anyone to really know Paul Eppinger. I resisted being open and vulnerable to anyone for fear that person would not like or accept what was found when he or she looked inside me.

And then a number of experiences collaborated to begin to break that shell. One was the marriage crisis that forced me to recognize my weaknesses and failures. Another involved the counseling sessions that allowed the counselor to help me discern what had led me to that point and also led him to accept me in all my hurt and pain at that point. Still another was sharing with Sybil, as honestly as I could, my deepest feelings, thoughts, desires, doubts, fantasies, and weaknesses—and having her accept me, love me, support me. Then I could begin to share myself with several other people whom I have learned to trust and have them love, accept, and support me in my needs. That is a giant step for this one small unit of humankind!

Such steps of vulnerability—at different levels and on different subjects with different people—have been part of my journey. But I'm in process, so I still get frightened about sharing who I really am. Like Jericho, however, the walls are crumbling. I am finding increasing strength in letting individuals and groups, including a loving congregation, know more and more who Paul Eppinger really is.

Scripture

And after she [Martha] had said this, she went back and called her sister Mary aside. "The Teacher is here," she said, "and is asking for you." When Mary heard this, she got up quickly and went to him. Now Jesus had not yet entered the village, but was still at the place where Martha had met him. When the Jews who had been with Mary in the house, comforting her, noticed how quickly she got up and went out, they followed her, supposing she was going to the tomb to mourn there.

When Mary reached the place where Jesus was and saw him, she fell at his feet and said, "Lord, if you had been here, my brother would not have died."

When Jesus saw her weeping, and the Jews who had come along with her also weeping, he was deeply moved in spirit and troubled.

"Where have you laid him?" he asked.

"Come and see, Lord," they replied.

Jesus wept.

Then the Jews said, "See how he loved him!"

But some of them said, "Could not he who opened the eyes of the blind man have kept this man from dying?"

John 11:28–37

Personal Notes

Further Insight

Do I dare find out who I really am? Have I let anyone else know who I really am? The lie we live is probably only a lie we tell ourselves. Most people who get close to us surely see more than we think but are too polite to tell us what they see.

The neighborhood bar is possibly the best counterfeit there is to the fellowship Christ wants to give his church. It's an imitation, dispensing liquor instead of grace, escape rather than reality, but it is a permissive, accepting, and inclusive fellowship. It is unshockable. It is democratic. You can tell people secrets and they usually don't tell others or even want to. The bar flourishes not because most people are alcoholics, but because God has put into the human heart the desire to know and be known, to love and be loved, and so many seek a counterfeit at the price of a few beers.

With all my heart I believe that Christ wants his church to be unshockable, democratic, permissive—a fellowship where people can come in and say, "I'm sunk!" "I'm beat!" "I've had it!" Alcoholics Anonymous has this quality. Our churches too often miss it.

The rebirth of a biblical theology in most of the major denominations today has resulted in a commitment-centered message. I genuinely rejoice in it, but it's not enough. One more altar call, decision card, church officers' retreat, or campfire surrender won't do it. Something else is needed. A fellowship must exist where committed people can begin to be honest with one another and discover the dimension of apostolic fellowship.

From Miller and Larson,
The Edge of Adventure, pp. 156–57.

Comments

Questions to Discuss

1. I feel free to share myself with one or more persons in our congregation in these ways . . .

2. Areas where I feel threatened by this are . . .

3. Places where I feel we can improve the openness, sharing, acceptance, and loving factor between us and members of the church are . . .

Our Prayer

O God, help us to break down our walls and become real people with those around us. Help us to be people who can share, laugh, and just be ourselves around our friends. . . .

Amen.

17

Living in a Fishbowl

Avoiding the Piranhas

PAUL and SYBIL:

We hadn't lived in our first parsonage a week when we learned that we were living in a fishbowl. Those walls and curtains that surrounded our living space were really totally transparent, and everybody in the community knew everything about our lives. There was no wiretapping, no eavesdropping. No, there was a far more effective surveillance system!

Her name was Sadie, and she lived right across the road from the church and parsonage. Sadie was in her seventies and had been sickly for thirty years. She left her house only to go to the doctor or to putter in her yard during late spring or early fall, when the weather was mild enough. Through the windows of her house, Sadie had direct visual access to everything that happened at the church or parsonage. She knew who came to church on Sunday morning, with whom they came, and what they wore; how well attended a meeting was; who visited us and how long they stayed; when we left the house and how long we were gone; and lots more. Another vital factor was that we were living out in the country and thus were on a four-party telephone line. This meant that one party could hear the phone conversations of the other three by lifting the receiver when someone else happened to be talking. However, each of us could hear only one other person's phone ring. And Sadie was the party whose ring we heard and who heard ours.

Our fishbowl existence was definitely confirmed when the two of us went away for most of a weekend to help lead a state youth convention. When we returned, some friends from out of state telephoned us. "When did you get home from your trip?" they inquired.

Puzzled at their question, we responded, "We arrived home Saturday night. But how did you know we were away?"

"Well, we tried to call you on Friday. When there was no answer, we assumed you were merely out for the evening and would be home on Saturday, preparing for your Sunday responsibilities. So we tried again Saturday morning and let the phone ring a long time. Finally, your neighbor answered and told us she didn't know where you were, but since both of you left on Friday with clothes hanging in the back of the car, you must be staying overnight." The fishbowl existence was a reality for us!

Anyone in a public position knows about the fishbowl syndrome. We felt it in our first pastorate in a rural community and have also experienced it in large churches in metropolitan areas. Lack of privacy is a given in our lives. To deal with this reality, we must first accept that it is an expected part of the life of anyone in the limelight. Sometimes being under observation can be affirming, supportive, and helpful. At other times, destructive piranhas are waiting to attack. In any case, we need to plan time and events where—as an individual, as a couple, and as a family—we can take time aside for private refreshment and relaxation. Besides that, a place should be reserved in the home as personal for each member. Even the youngest should have an opportunity for privacy when it is needed and desired. We all need the privilege of escaping the fishbowl and moving to our own point of solitude at will.

Scripture   **Personal Notes**

As soon as they left the synagogue, they went with James and John to the home of Simon and Andrew. Simon's mother-in-law was in bed with a fever, and they told Jesus about her. So he went to her, took her hand and helped her up. The fever left her and she began to wait on them.

That evening after sunset the people brought to Jesus all the sick and demon-possessed. The whole town gathered at the door, and Jesus healed many who had various diseases. He also drove out many demons, but he would not let the demons speak because they knew who he was.

Very early in the morning, while it was still dark, Jesus got up, left the

house and went off to a solitary place,
where he prayed.

                                    Mark 1:29–35

Further Insight

What is essential about me? Well, I
think what is essential is that I live
and embrace life *right now,* wherever
I am. I grab it in my arms! Don't spend
time crying about yesterday—yesterday is over with! I forgive my past. I
forgive the people who've hurt me. I
don't want to spend the rest of my life
blaming and pointing a finger. . . .

Can you forgive? . . . Can you say
it's "OK?" Can you say, "They are
people, too?" and you take them in
your arms and embrace them? Then
take your *self* in your arms. Find out
again that you *are* special, that you *are*
unique, that you are wondrous, that in
all the world there is only *one* of you!
Hug yourself, you sweet old thing!

Sure you've screwed up, and sometimes you do dumb things and you
forget that you are a human being, but
the most wonderful thing about you is
that, no matter where you are, you
have potential to grow. You are just
starting. . . .

Nikos Kazantzakis says, "You have
your brush, you have your colors, *you*
paint paradise, then in you go." Do it!!
Take orange and magenta and blue
and purple . . . and green, and
yellow—and paint your paradise. You
can *do* that! You can do it right now.
It's your life that is essential.

As long as you learn, as long as
you're willing to take your life in your
hands, and kiss it and go on from
there. Then there is growth. Then
there is life!

From Buscaglia,
Living, Loving & Learning, pp. 77–79.

Comments

Questions to Discuss

1. I feel invaded in our fishbowl existence when . . .

2. I feel affirmed by the people around us when . . .

3. I think we can handle our fishbowl lives better by . . .

Our Prayer

O God, we know that Jesus lived in a fishbowl, yet he took time to be by himself to think, pray, laugh, and play. Help us to have the courage to do the same thing. . . .

Amen.

18

Managing the Clock's Demands

"Mommy, Mommy the pastor is here!"

SYBIL:

We should have known we were in trouble one day within the first five years of our marriage, when our first daughter was three years old. I had taught our children from the time they began to toddle to run to the door and greet their daddy with a hug and a kiss whenever he came home. It was always a high point of the day, emphasizing the importance of love, affection, touching, and talking, as well as of greetings and goodbyes.

In those early years of ministry, people in the church called Paul either by his first name or by the title *Pastor*, so somewhere along the line our three-year-old had established the fact that her daddy was known by that term. Since this was an exciting, growing, busy congregation, church-related events more and more captured Paul's time and attention. On this particular day, as he moved from his car to the door of our home at lunchtime, our little girl looked out the door and then came running to me in the kitchen, exclaiming, "Mommy, Mommy, the pastor is here!" We laughed at the time, and Paul tried to reassure her that he was her daddy, not just "the pastor."

PAUL:

The message was unmistakably there: I was spending too much of my time away from home—too much time serving other people, too much time doing pastoral duties, too much time involved with the community. All of these demands were limiting my time with my family.

It takes time to build the spousal relationship and to develop relation-

92

ships with one's children. Often, the time a person gives to a job comes from inner pressures—the need to please everyone, the desire to produce and be considered successful, or the fear of not being tapped for new career opportunities. Such pressures can seriously damage family relationships, even in the ministry where home life has always been highly valued.

Critical decisions are involved when balancing the time required for the job and the time required to build and deepen family relationships. Far too often, we in the ministry are weighed in the balance and found wanting, simply because we can't handle the clock's incessant demands.

Scripture

As Jesus and his disciples were on their way, he came to a village where a woman named Martha opened her home to him. She had a sister called Mary, who sat at the Lord's feet listening to what he said. But Martha was distracted by all the preparations that had to be made. She came to him and asked, "Lord, don't you care that my sister has left me to do the work by myself? Tell her to help me!"

"Martha, Martha," the Lord answered, "you are worried and upset about many things, but only one thing is needed. Mary has chosen what is better, and it will not be taken away from her."

Luke 10:38–42

Personal Notes

Further Insight

Most people can tell you with a straight face that the pressures they feel are the result of temporary circumstances. Their future will be less hectic. A slower day is coming. A light shines at the end of the dark tunnel. Unfortunately, their optimism is usually unjustified. It is my observation that the hoped for period of tranquility rarely arrives. Instead, these short term pressures have a way of becoming sandwiched back to back,

Comments

so that families emerge from one crisis and sail directly into another. Thus, we live our entire lives in the fast lane, hurtling down the road toward heart failure. We have deluded ourselves into believing that circumstances have forced us to work too hard for a short time, when, in fact, we are driven from within. We lack the discipline to limit our entanglements with the world, choosing instead to be dominated by our work and the materialistic gadgetry it will bring. And what is sacrificed in the process are the loving relationships with wives and children and friends who give life meaning.

From Dobson,
Straight Talk to Men and Their Wives, p. 139.

Questions to Discuss

1. As I look at my calendar or date book for the past month, I find I have spent most of my time in these ways:

2. I wish I could spend my time . . .

3. We can reorganize our time to make our dreams become reality by . . .

Our Prayer

O God, realizing that time is one great factor that can never be recovered, help us so to use our days that we might "redeem the times" in our relationship. . . .

Amen.

19

Time and Priorities

". . . I wish I could take a day off each week."

PAUL:

I thought I had learned my lesson about managing time and setting correct priorities for its use, but there I was—trapped! One of our daughters was celebrating a birthday, and I was out of town for a speaking commitment that had been scheduled months in advance. Although I had been looking forward to the occasion, now my joy changed to sorrow. I was in the wrong place at the wrong time, unable to do anything about it. Since then, I've changed my approach to time scheduling by writing birthdays and other important family dates on my calendar in advance so that nothing preempts them.

I know that other pastors face the dilemma of juggling their available time, because some have sought me out for counseling about various problems. One had been coming to me for several weeks. At the close of a session, we were discussing when we could get together again. When he suggested a week from the coming Monday, I responded by saying, "I'm sorry, but Monday is my day off and I don't schedule anything on that day." He stopped, looked wistful for a moment, and then said, "Paul, I wish I could take a day off each week." I responded, "Bill, the church you pastor has about a hundred members, and the town you are serving is a small one. It's not your church or community that is preventing you from taking a day off. It's *you*!"

For many of us who are pastors, the monkey we carry on our backs is not the church's demands but our own workaholism. We seem to feel that by giving more and more to our church, we will somehow be more revered by our people and more assured of heaven. It is as if we were saying, "Look how much we are sacrificing of ourselves for our calling!" But most people in our congregations want us to have some free time, especially time with our spouses and children. It is up to us to take that time and arrange our schedules accordingly, even if that means marking on our calendars a year in advance our important family days. We *can* say no to other people and demands and assign top priority to time for our own enrichment, for the strengthening of our marriages, and for experiences with our children. For example, a couple of years ago a professor in a Kansas City seminary asked me to lecture to one of his Monday classes. It was a special family day, so I told him I could not make it because of that commitment. He told his class that and later declared to me, "That was the best lesson you could have taught!" I am grateful he has reminded me of that from time to time.

Scripture

There is a time for everything, and a season for every activity under heaven: a time to be born and a time to die, a time to plant and a time to uproot, a time to kill and a time to heal, a time to tear down and a time to build, a time to weep and a time to laugh, a time to mourn and a time to dance, a time to scatter stones and a time to gather them, a time to embrace and a time to refrain, a time to search and a time to give up, a time to keep and a time to throw away, a time to tear and a time to mend, a time to be silent and a time to speak, a time to love and a time to hate, a time for war and a time for peace.

What does the worker gain from his toil?

Ecclesiastes 3:1–9

Further Insight

Continuing physical and emotional contact is essential to a vital marriage. But the quality of that contact is as important as its quantity. Filling your days with too much activity, shared or otherwise, can cause tension and

Personal Notes

Comments

fatigue to undermine the time you spend together. So often we save our best efforts and energies for "outsiders" and give each other the dregs that remain. True, home should be a refuge from life's pressures, a place where you can "let go" and "let down." But if all that a husband and wife gets from each other is an exhausted zombie or a complaining bundle of nerves, it's not fair.

The quality of a couple's time together is directly proportionate to a number of "hook-up points"—shared interests—that link their lives. That's why growing apart is such a major marital problem—especially for older couples who no longer have what might be the built-in hook-up points of children, homebuilding, job advancement. A couple can try to remedy this by scheduling more shared time. But without mutual interests that time often proves boring, tense, even anxiety-producing.

From Lasswell and Lobsenz,
No Fault Marriage, pp. 234-35.

Questions to Discuss

1. For me, our highest-quality contact points are . . .

2. The five most important things I would like to do with you that take time are . . .

3. To make time for these items, I know I'll have to readjust my schedule by . . .

Our Prayer

O God, help us to prioritize our time so our lives will be focused, yet calm; exciting, yet not anxious; progressive, yet not hectic. . . .

Amen.

20

A Matter of Balance

"Dumb dog! Doesn't even know how to love!"

SYBIL:

Cleopatra was her name, and she was the seventh member of our family. "Cleo" weighed in at about seventy-five pounds and had the massive frame that characterizes an English bulldog. She was gentle, quiet, tender. Yet, she had some of the other bulldog qualities, such as snorting when she breathed, drooling when she slept, and nipping at people's toes when she was playing. One day our youngest daughter, then about the age of four, was trying to play quietly with Cleo, but our dog was not in the mood for relaxation. The bright sun streaming through the window seemed to invigorate her, so she bounced around, nipping at Monica and trying to instigate a tug of war. Monica did everything she could to get Cleo to quiet down. She stroked gently, but Cleo cavorted like a circus pony. She talked soothingly, but Cleo growled and yipped. Our daughter's efforts to get her under control were met with absolutely no success. Finally, with great disgust, Monica declared, "Dumb dog! Doesn't even know how to love!"

There are a lot of us in the ministry who seem to go through that kind of experience. We are just like Cleo. We can't seem to find the correct balance between play, work, and rest. When we have tensions from the problems of others, we seek to share their burdens. We walk with our parishioners through deep distress; death, divorce, and disaster are part of our regular experiences. Because we work for a caregiving organization, we very often burn out or become discouraged at the magnitude of our task. Consequently, we sometimes get to be people who move around in a dejected state of life—either grunting and growling at everyone around us or sleeping dazedly in the sun. Too often, we don't even respond to our family in the way they need us to at that time—we don't seem to know how to love.

But the correct balance must be found if we are to keep the tensions of our work from exhausting us. We need time for personal reading and reflection, time for physical activities (tennis, golf, running), time for sleeping and goofing off, time for hobbies, time to be with the family, time to make love, time to travel. These personal times of "recreation" are literally for re-creation, for thereby the tensions of our work can be counterbalanced by meeting our own needs. Our own lives will be made whole again, and we will be relearning how to love those closest to us.

Scripture

Dear friends, let us love one another, for love comes from God. Everyone who loves has been born of God and knows God. Whoever does not love does not know God, because God is love. This is how God showed his love among us: He sent his one and only Son into the world that we might live through him. This is love: not that we loved God, but that he loved us and sent his Son as an atoning sacrifice for our sins. Dear friends, since God so loved us, we also ought to love one another. No one has ever seen God; but if we love one another, God lives in us and his love is made complete in us. . . .

And so we know and rely on the love God has for us. God is love. Whoever lives in love lives in God, and God in him.

1 John 4:7–12, 16

Personal Notes

Further Insight

More than ten years ago I went through an extremely painful process of self-examination, when I realized how great a part pride had been playing in my religious and church life. I had fought zealously for truth and

Comments

spiritual revival in the Church, I had taken the initiative in a large number of activities, and made many speeches; and the pride of being a champion of truth, I fully realized now, had been what spurred me on, rather than the love of men's souls. That day I resolved to remain quiet, to get on with my own humble affairs. I turned down requests to take on responsibilities and to give lectures. I soon realized, however, that now I was being just as proud in refusing these things. Pride was reappearing in a new guise: that of having had a profound experience of self-examination. I felt desperate. I saw that whatever I did, whether I spoke or remained silent, the cunning enemy would always be there. I had gone down into a tunnel that led to a blank wall. In my despair I asked a young pastor, whom I hardly knew, how one could become a leader of men without sinking into the morass of pride. I must have looked particularly strained, because the pastor replied: "My dear doctor, you must first learn to smile!"

I have to admit that I found this reply excessively irritating. I felt that the pastor was laughing at me and at my worry. I felt that in the words of the Gospel I had asked for bread and had been given a stone. Furthermore, it so happened that I could not stand people who talked about their religion with complacent smiles on their faces. They were so smug and superficial. Only when I got home did I see the light. There came into my mind the simple thought that the opposite of the smiling attitude is the serious one, and I suddenly realized how seriously I had been taking myself, with my "problem" of pride, instead of simply confessing it and leaving it all up to God. I saw that what was getting me down was not so much my pride as my shame at being proud, and that other utopian pride which consists in trying to solve on one's own a problem which no man can solve. I began to smile at the thought that it was just in order to relieve me of that impossible and crushing burden that Christ came and died. . . .

Two or three years after the pastor had urged me to smile, there came a certain man into my study. "I have come to thank you," he said, "for having led me to Jesus." "But I don't remember ever having seen you before!" "No doubt, but I have seen you, and all at once, when I saw you smiling all by yourself, I said to myself that Christian life must be worth it."

From Tournier,
The Person Reborn, pp. 205–7.

Questions to Discuss

1. Ways I have found release from my work tensions are . . .

2. Ways I have seen you enjoying recreation and finding release from your tensions are . . .

3. I'd like for us together to make our leisure time an experience for building intimacy by . . .

Our Prayer

O God, because you have mandated us to love, help us to find the balance we need to see you more clearly, love you more dearly, follow you more nearly, and—out of that experience—to love each other with excitement and joy. . . .

Amen.

21

Self-Determination and the Spouse's Role

"Honey, you don't have to be an example for the whole church!"

SYBIL:

We had been married about eight years. We had both come into our marriage and into the pastorate with a driving desire to be the best that we could possibly be. Somehow that "best" evolved into a "be perfect" syndrome. For the first two years, Paul was in graduate school and I was teaching school. Besides those tasks, we pastored a wonderful rural church. We both put in long and hard hours to help that church become the best *it* could be.

Paul was called to a suburban church when his seminary education was completed. He threw his total being into that job, too. Shortly after we began our ministry in that church, our first baby arrived. Within five years we had four babies—and I was still striving for perfection in everything. Within a week after each baby was born, that baby and I (and her sisters, after the second) were attending church services, not only on Sunday morning, but Sunday evening and Wednesday night. There were also women's meetings and many other special church functions to attend. I was desperately seeking to be the ideal minister's wife. It finally almost exhausted me emotionally, spiritually, and physically.

That is when "Grandma Hampson" entered the picture. She was a cheerful, active member of our church. Since our families were a thousand miles away, Grandma Hampson had become a surrogate grandmother for our family. Quiet, gentle, loving, with the wisdom of a sage, she gave all of us great strength. One day Grandma Hampson very quietly but firmly said to me, "Honey, you don't have to be an example for the whole church!"

Somehow, those were the very words I needed to hear, and two things began to happen. First, I began to shed the "be perfect" syndrome, to move away from the "super helpmate" role and instead be a mother and a wife who was satisfied with who she was. That meant accepting that I did not have to fit every church member's idea as to what a minister's spouse should be. Second, no longer did I have to be at every meeting, at every choir practice, at every service. I was back on the road to being a person instead of playing an impossible role that was destroying my entire family, including myself! I realized that spouses have had their individualized purposes, from biblical times until the present.

Scripture	Personal Notes

The body is a unit, though it is made up of many parts; and though all its parts are many, they form one body. So it is with Christ. For we were all baptized by one Spirit into one body—whether Jews or Greeks, slave or free—and we were all given the one Spirit to drink.

Now you are the body of Christ, and each one of you is a part of it. And in the church God has appointed first of all apostles, second prophets, third teachers, then workers of miracles, also those having gifts of healing, those able to help others, those with gifts of administration, and those speaking in different kinds of tongues. Are all apostles? Are all prophets? Are all teachers? Do all work miracles? Do all have gifts of healing? Do all speak in tongues? Do all interpret? But eagerly desire the greater gifts. And now I will show you the most excellent way.

If I speak in the tongues of men and of angels, but have not love, I am only a resounding gong or a clanging cymbal.

And now these three remain: faith,

hope and love. But the greatest of these is love.

1 Corinthians 12:12–13, 27–31; 13:1, 13

Further Insight

Each of us is a separate person. We are the subtle combination of factors which are never likely to occur again. We are all singular and incomparable. Who and what we are has been determined largely by our heredity, society, education, family, and friends. All of these have helped to make our lives richer and more exciting. But they have also brought with them complications, frustrations, and contradictions which have made severe demands upon our mental and emotional energies and which are likely to continue to do so in the future. It was in this way that our personhood was created, both by the rich and exciting as well as the frustrating and depressing. Somewhere, within and between both, will lie our true selves.

As fully functioning persons we know that we have a right to be what we are, even if what we are is not compatible with what we have learned to be. We have a right to choose our own selves, even if that self is different from the selves of others. We have the right to feel as we do even if those feelings are frowned upon by others. This does not mean that we have a right to inflict ourselves upon others any more than we would desire to have others inflict themselves upon us. It does mean that we have a right to choose, develop and live congruently with ourselves and to share without apology.

From Buscaglia, *Personhood*, p. 100.

Comments

Questions to Discuss

1. My expectations of me in our marriage are . . .

2. My expectations of you in our marriage are . . .

3. My expectations of our marriage in relationship to our professions are . . .

Our Prayer

O God, help me to be true to myself while at the same time being loving and helpful to my spouse. Bless our relationship together, for your great glory and our great good. . . .

Amen.

22

Spouses and the Broader "Ministry"

"I call my wife 'the Bishop'!"

PAUL:

It happened in a support group of ministers in which I was involved. We had been together for several months and had had the exciting opportunity of beginning to share who we were, how we felt about a lot of things, what we believed, and where we hurt—all in an atmosphere of trust. On this particular day, we were talking about our marriages, and when it came to one particular new friend, he said, "I call my wife 'the Bishop'!" Then his voice began to rise as he said, "Every day she tells me who to call on, which hospital to visit, what to preach, and where to go." He went on to tell us that in her teenage years his wife had felt a deep desire to go into the ministry. Because, in that day and in that denomination, women were not allowed to be ordained, she had done the next best thing: she had found a man going into the ministry and had married him. Now she was living out her frustrated call to the ministry by dictating to her husband everything he was to do. She had not married the man, she had married the profession. This obviously set up all sorts of competitive situations and made for an interplay of harassment and domination.

Today there are a myriad of opportunities for nonordained spouses. Some are college professors; others are marriage-and-family counselors. Some teach aerobic dancing; others are active in politics. Some have professions that are closely related to ministry. Others' jobs are a world apart. In a deep sense, all are fulfilling their own "ministry" in their own special way. Another option some spouses have taken is to get the training, become ordained, and move into professional ministry themselves, some in a co-pastoral situation and others in a totally different church.

The traditional role for a pastor's spouse of a past generation involved some rather circumscribed responsibilities in the local congregation. That is still a viable option for many, so many spouses are strengthening the Sunday school or other church organizations, visiting the elderly and sick, or being involved with the youth of the church.

It is possible for a balance to be established so that each person in a marriage can have a life of fulfillment, freedom, and joy under God and at the same time move together in an exciting, growing, cooperative relationship. This opportunity can be found in any marriage where love and mutual respect have become habitual.

Scripture   ## Personal Notes

Deborah, a prophetess, the wife of Lappidoth, was leading Israel at that time. She held court under the Palm of Deborah between Ramah and Bethel in the hill country of Ephraim, and the Israelites came to her to have their disputes decided. She sent for Barak son of Abinoam from Kedesh in Naphtali and said to him, "The LORD, the God of Israel, commands you: 'Go, take with you ten thousand men of Naphtali and Zebulun and lead the way to Mount Tabor. I will lure Sisera, the commander of Jabin's army, with his chariots and his troops to the Kishon River and give him into your hands.'"

Barak said to her, "If you go with me, I will go; but if you don't go with me, I won't go."

"Very well," Deborah said, "I will go with you. But because of the way you are going about this, the honor will not be yours, for the Lord will hand Sisera over to a woman." So Deborah went with Barak to Kedesh, where he summoned Zebulun and Naphtali. Ten thousand men followed him, and Deborah also went with him.

Judges 4:4–10

Further Insight   Comments

The Real Me

I like the feel of the real me . . .
   the feel of spiritual steel,
   the feel of God and Truth and
      Christ
   in the real me.
I like the feel of the real me . . .
   the feel of unlimited potential
   the feel of untapped love and
      faith and life
   in the real me.
I like the feel of the real me . . .
   the feel of strength, purpose,
      direction,
   the feel of great health and
      wealth,
   the feel of awakening joy,
      peace, freedom
   in the real me.
I like the feel of the real me . . .
   the feel of wholeness and one-
      ness,
   the feel of unity with God and
      with man
   in the real me.
I like the feel of the real me . . .
   and I like what happens to me
      and in me
   as I accept, appreciate and affirm
   the real me.

From March 1976 *Unity Magazine,*
quoted by J. Sig Paulsen

Questions to Discuss

1. I feel supported by you in my profession when you . . .

2. I would like to support you more in your profession by . . .

3. I wish you would support me more by . . .

Our Prayer

O God, help us in our ministries: to fulfill our own, to support each other, and to discover the unique opportunity to serve you, which is ours as a couple. . . .

Amen.

23

The Role of the Pastor's Family

"Mommy, do I have to go to church tonight?"

SYBIL:

It was our church's annual "School of Missions." The effort of many people had gone into its preparation. Among other things, on this particular Sunday evening we were going to be viewing a documentary film on "Hunger in America."

Shortly before time to leave home for the service, our then eleven-year-old daughter came to me pleading, "Mommy, do I have to go to church tonight?" Since church attendance was not a debatable issue in our home, I was very much surprised by this query from our serious-minded child, who regularly accompanied me to every service.

"Are you sick?" I asked.

"No," came the answer.

"Then why do you not want to go to church tonight?"

"Mommy, I've been watching TV reports of the earthquake in South America this afternoon. I've seen parents whose children are missing, the crying and hungry children who can't find their homes or families, and the devastation of their entire city. Now I'm supposed to go to church and watch a movie about hungry poor people and old people and children with no money to buy school lunches when everybody else is eating. Why do we make ourselves feel bad about other people's needs every year when it doesn't change anything and we don't do anything different? I don't want to see any more suffering tonight!"

Needless to say, I agreed she could stay home that evening. Her comments were a strong indictment of our level of response to human need. While we contributed rather generously from our family income to mission programs, we had not involved our family decision making and lifestyle in the process.

The following evening our family discussed the situation and together decided to fast every Tuesday evening and contribute what we normally spend on a family meal to a hunger program. This practice continued for many years throughout the time our children were at home.

Though it is sometimes difficult to realize that our children might have different priorities from our own, the exciting truth is that—more than being *our* children—they are God's children and need the freedom to respond to God in their own way. Sometimes they can be our teachers, if we stay open to that possibility by asking questions, listening to their answers, and learning from them. Children play an important part in our own spiritual growth and in our ministry. They can lead us into new facets of spiritual truth, sometimes challenging our concern with the planned programs of the church and "what other people might think" to confront us with the heart of the gospel.

Scripture   ## Personal Notes

Every year his [Jesus'] parents went to Jerusalem for the Feast of the Passover. When he was twelve years old, they went up to the Feast, according to the custom. After the Feast was over, while his parents were returning home, the boy Jesus stayed behind in Jerusalem, but they were unaware of it. Thinking he was in their company, they traveled on for a day. Then they began looking for him among their relatives and friends. When they did not find him, they went back to Jerusalem to look for him. After three days they found him in the temple courts, sitting among the teachers, listening to them and asking them questions. Everyone who heard him was amazed at his understanding and his answers. When his parents saw him, they were astonished. His mother said to him, "Son, why have you treated us like this? Your father and I have been anxiously searching for you."

"Why were you searching for me?"

he asked. "Didn't you know I had to be in my Father's house?" But they did not understand what he was saying to them.

Then he went down to Nazareth with them and was obedient to them. But his mother treasured all these things in her heart. And Jesus grew in wisdom and stature, and in favor with God and men.

Luke 2:41–52

Further Insight

"What Every Child Needs"

To grow healthy and strong, children should have good food, plenty of sleep, exercise and fresh air. Children have emotional needs, too. To have good health—to be both healthy and happy—all children require:

Love

Every child needs to feel loved
    and wanted.
    that he matters very much to
        someone.
    that there are people near
        him who care what
        happens to him.

Security

Every child needs to know
    that her home is a good safe
        place she can feel sure
        about.
    that her parents or other
        protective adults will
        always be on hand,
        especially in times of
        crisis when she needs
        them most.
    that she belongs to a group;
    that there is a place where
        she fits in.

Comments

Acceptance

Every child needs to believe
  that she is liked for herself,
    just the way she is.
  that she is liked all the time,
    and not only when she
    acts according to others'
    ideas of the way a child
    should act.
  that she is always accepted,
    even though others may
    not approve of the things
    she does.
  that she will be able to grow
    and develop in her own
    way.

Control

Every child needs to know
  that there are limits to what
    he is permitted to do and
    that he will be held to
    these limits.
  that though it is all right to
    feel jealous or angry, he
    will not be allowed to hurt
    himself or others when he
    has these feelings.

Guidance

Every child needs to have
  friendly help in learning how
    to behave toward persons
    and things.
  adults around him to show
    him by example how to
    get along with others.

Independence

Every child needs to know
  that she will be encouraged
    to try new things and to
    grow.

that there is confidence in her
and her ability to do
things for herself and by
herself

Protection

Every child needs to feel
that she will be kept safe
from harm.
that when she must face
strange, unknown and
frightening situations,
someone will be there to
help.

Faith

Every child needs to have
a set of moral standards to
live by.
a belief in the human values—kindness, courage,
honesty, generosity, and
justice.

From National Mental Health Association.

Questions to Discuss

1. The hurts, joys, dreams, and fears of each of my children that I know and accept are . . .

2. Three things I would like to share with my children so they can know me better are . . .

3. I pledge to write or tell each member of my family the following affirmation within the next twenty-four hours:

Our Prayer

O God, help me not to make my children an extension of my ego. Show me how I can allow and help them to be what you desire for them to be—total human beings. . . .

Amen.

24

"Preacher's Kids"—
Weighing Expectations

"I get so tired of people invading our family life!"

SYBIL:

Like parents everywhere, Paul and I have always wanted life's best for our children. We wanted them to be people of faith, and still want this. The very names of our daughters are faith names: Damaris, Priscilla, Stephanie Joy, and Monica Elizabeth. Attendance at church and Sunday school was always a high point in the week. We tried to make Sunday morning a joyful experience.

When the children were young, Paul let them take turns going with him early on Sunday mornings to check on things at the church. He allowed each one to "help drive the car" on those trips. Sunday dinner was a special occasion in the dining room, complete with china, crystal, silver, and often invited guests. Our church family helped by giving the children attention, affirmation, and nurturing.

Then the confusion began. Even though we did not want to restrict our children unnecessarily, we did have certain expectations of them. When they were unable to meet our standards, we felt threatened. The children began to ask questions about why their friends could do all kinds of other things on Sundays while they were locked into the church program. And, as much as they tried to escape it, they were still known as "preacher's kids," both within and outside the church. It's as though that was emblazoned on their foreheads for everyone to see; no matter how hard they tried, they could not avoid that mark. The congregation, we as parents, and often even the community at large seemed to have a certain set of expectations for them.

Then came the mixture of acceptance and rejection, accepting the faith and love and power of God, yet feeling angry over the demands of the ministry—telephone calls during dinner, meetings their parents attended in the evenings, people coming to the house to see the pastor. "I get so tired of people invading our family life! Why can't they leave us alone? Why can't we be like everybody else?" is the way one of our children once expressed it. What an excitement that family life was that important to her, but what a perplexity!

We have done a number of things in an attempt to balance the situation. We have always sought to build a relationship with our congregations so they would understand and support our dilemma, just as we seek to understand and support them. We have sought to be open with our children so that we can discuss our anxieties and concerns, as well as the joys and advantages of being people of faith in leadership positions. Through the years we have done a variety of practical things: taking the telephone off the hook during dinner, engaging an answering service, getting the family away on picnics, outings, and family vacations.

All of this has had an impact on our children. The same daughter who once complained about being "invaded" recently said, "I'm glad we have had people in for Sunday dinner often. I've met so many interesting people, have learned a lot from them, and I'm also comfortable now when I'm with strangers or at a very formal dinner. My friends ask *me* which fork to use!"

Scripture

Paul, an apostle of Christ Jesus by the will of God, according to the promise of life that is in Christ Jesus.

To Timothy, my dear son: Grace, mercy and peace from God the Father and Christ Jesus our Lord.

I thank God, whom I serve, as my forefathers did, with a clear conscience, as night and day I constantly remember you in my prayers. Recalling your tears, I long to see you, so that I may be filled with joy. I have been reminded of your sincere faith, which first lived in your grandmother Lois and in your mother Eunice and, I am persuaded, now lives in you also. For this reason I remind you to fan

Personal Notes

into flame the gift of God, which is in you through the laying on of my hands. For God did not give us a spirit of timidity, but a spirit of power, of love and of self-discipline.

2 Timothy 1:1–7

Train a child in the way he should go, and when he is old he will not turn from it.

Proverbs 22:6

Further Insight

Dr. Edward A. Strecker, a psychiatrist, tells of a father, a very wealthy man in a high government post, who came to his office one day.

"I have two sons," he said briskly, "and they are fine boys but a little wild. Always getting expelled from school and that sort of thing. They need a father's guidance. Their mother is a good woman and loves them very much, but she spoils them. I'm afraid they won't grow up to be real men.

"Unfortunately, I can't spend much time with them for I have had to put my duty to the nation before everything else. My idea is that you, in effect, should be their father. Take full charge. I'll pay you anything you ask. It would be worth a great deal to me to know that my boys were in your care."

Regretfully, I had to say no. "It's not that I don't want the job," I told him. "Your boys need a father all right, but no substitute will do. It seems to me your first responsibility to this country is to develop your sons into upstanding, well-balanced, responsible young citizens. Nothing you accomplish in Washington can possibly be more important!"

Comments

After I turned down his suggestion, he insisted on sending his sons to a strict boys' school in order, as he put it, "that they might be exposed to strong male influences." The school was a good one, but teachers, however conscientious, cannot substitute for a father. The boys were even then struggling with emotional problems caused mainly by their lopsided family life.

At school, they developed further difficulties that would have been instantly apparent to the watchful eye of a father but went unnoticed by the indulgent mother and busy teachers. The boys are now 17 and 19. The younger is a drug addict, struggling with serious problems of adjustment that verge on homosexuality. The other is a thief. Even his influential father will not be able to keep him out of prison much longer.

Children need a father. . . . The society your child is destined to grow up in is both male and female. Your son needs a man around that he can respect and imitate. Daughters need a father, too. . . . Better than any lectures about being home at a reasonable hour, being selective about the choice of friends, and being clean and pure of body is the example of a father who is all of these things.

From Myers,
Happiness Is Still Homemade, pp. 77–79.

Questions to Discuss

1. Every day, I think I really listen to my children by . . .

2. When our children leave our home as adults, three qualities or character traits I would most like for them to have are . . .

3. Ways we need to adjust our lives to give quality time, energy, teaching, and love to our children are . . .

Our Prayer

O God, help us to see that committee meetings, choir practices, and sermon preparations go on forever, but that we have our children with us for only a few short, select years. Help us to make the right choices for their benefit when they are young and to teach them how to make their own right choices later on. . . .

Amen.

25

Divorce as an Option

"'til death do us part"?

PAUL:

"You *do* have an option," our counselor said to us, though we had never felt as if we had any choice but to stay together. We had come into this marriage "'til death do us part." Divorce had never been a part of our background, training, thoughts, or anticipation. We believed we were in this marriage forever. But, during the last several months, conditions had deteriorated to such an extent that marriage was painful at best and destructive for each of us at worst. To compound the pain and frustration, we had not seen any way out. When we are young adults, death seems years away, and "'til death do us part" seems like forever! We had been verbalizing our pain, our concern, and our frustration to the counselor when he responded, "You *do* have an option." We immediately asked what the option was, and our counselor very quietly and wisely said, "Divorce! You really can terminate your marriage."

Gradually and ironically, as the reality of that truth hit us, both Sybil and I felt a new optimism for our marriage. The realization that we were not locked into an entirely destructive relationship gave us a hope that our marriage really could be an exciting, growing, creative experience. An ancient Greek axiom states, "Never corner an enemy so that he has no avenue of escape, because when he is cornered he will fight to the death and kill you. But, if he has an avenue of escape through which he can move and somehow preserve his life, his honor, and integrity, he will live to be your friend." That's what happened to us. Much of the pressure we had felt to make our marriage a flawless success was released when we realized that divorce could be an option. It allowed us the joy and the power to recognize our weaknesses, affirm our own lives, and enjoy one another in a new and creative way. We chose to stay in the marriage because of our love and commitment to the relationship, not because social custom prohibited any other option.

Scripture

A proclamation was then issued throughout Judah and Jerusalem for all the exiles to assemble in Jerusalem. Anyone who failed to appear within three days would forfeit all his property, in accordance with the decision of the officials and elders, and would himself be expelled from the assembly of the exiles.

Within the three days, all the men of Judah and Benjamin had gathered in Jerusalem. And on the twentieth day of the ninth month, all the people were sitting in the square before the house of God, greatly distressed by the occasion and because of the rain. Then Ezra the priest stood up and said to them, "You have been unfaithful; you have married foreign women, adding to Israel's guilt. Now make confession to the LORD, the God of your fathers, and do his will. Separate yourselves from the peoples around you and from your foreign wives."

Ezra 10:7–11

Further Insight

Today I look back on the last three years as the most personally enriching period of my life. Through a painful emotional crisis, I have become a happier and stronger person than I was before. I learned that what I went through was what all divorced people, men and women, go through to a greater or lesser degree—first a recognition that a relationship has died, then a period of mourning, and finally

Personal Notes

Comments

a slow, painful, emotional readjust-
ment to the facts of single life. I experienced the pitfalls along the way—the
wallowing in self pity, the refusal to let
go of the old relationship, the repeti-
tion of old ways in relating to new
people, the confusion of past emotions
with present reality—and I emerged
the better for it.

As a professional counselor and a
divorced man, I saw divorce as an
emotional process with its own inter-
nal time schedule that a divorce
decree can hasten or delay, but not
eradicate. It is a crisis that must be
lived through. More than that, however, more than just a time for picking
up the pieces, divorce is a new opportunity to improve on the past and create a fuller life—if you can come to
terms with the past, recognize self-
defeating behavior, and be willing to
change it.

From Krantzler,
Creative Divorce, pp. 27–28.

Questions to Discuss

1. For me, the factors that keep us from divorcing are . . .

2. For me, the factors that would cause me to want to end our marriage are . . .

3. The strengths in our relationship that I want to improve are . . .

Our Prayer

O God, just as you gave biblical people options in their lives, give us eyes to see our options and the wisdom to choose the ones best for us. . . .

Amen.

26

Facing Up to a Limited Salary

"It costs nothing to walk in the snow together!"

PAUL and SYBIL:
We have replayed this scenario many times as we think of the limited salary that most ministers receive. Imagine there is a doctor and his wife living in one house, and next door there is a minister and his wife. One day, the doctor's wife comes to him and says, "Sweetheart, I think our marriage is in trouble. I very seldom see you. You are working seventy hours a week, and I really wish we could spend more time together." The doctor responds, "But look at the big cars out there in the driveway; look at our membership in the country club; look at that trip we just took to Hawaii. I'm working all of those hours so that you can have all of these beautiful things." To which the doctor's wife replies, "I don't care about 'things.' I want *you*, so I want us to spend more time together. I want us to communicate, to spend time doing things with each other, to take time to get to know each other more deeply and develop our relationship." The doctor then has the choice of his wife or his "things." She has already made her choice—and it is her husband.

Next door, the minister's wife comes to him and says, "Sweetheart, I think our marriage is in trouble. I never get to see you; you are working seventy hours a week, and I really wish we could spend more time together and build a closer relationship." To which the minister responds, simply but emphatically, "I am doing the work of the Lord." The minister's wife is not battling a new Cadillac or a trip to Hawaii. She seems to be in mortal combat with the Almighty, and there is virtually no contest. She feels she is a loser before the conflict begins.

Although our churches have not always been as sensitive as they could

128

be to the material needs of the minister and family, we dare not use our ministerial calling (with its limited salary) as a cop-out for relationships. Since ministers are on a fixed salary, working longer hours does not provide additional income. At the same time, a heavy work schedule does not necessarily indicate a greater commitment to the kingdom, nor does it influence God's exercise of grace toward us. From the standpoint of time together, it is not money or lack of it that is the problem. Attitude is what counts. It doesn't cost very much money to go on a picnic or throw a Frisbee in the park, or sit and quietly talk with each other. These are the makings of a stronger relationship. It costs nothing to walk in the snow together!

Scripture

"No one can serve two masters. Either he will hate the one and love the other, or he will be devoted to the one and despise the other. You cannot serve both God and Money.

"Therefore I tell you, do not worry about your life, what you will eat or drink; or about your body, what you will wear. Is not life more important than food, and the body more important than clothes? Look at the birds of the air; they do not sow or reap or store away in barns, and yet your heavenly Father feeds them. Are you not much more valuable than they? Who of you by worrying can add a single hour to his life?

"And why do you worry about clothes? See how the lilies of the field grow. They do not labor or spin. Yet I tell you that not even Solomon in all his splendor was dressed like one of these. If that is how God clothes the grass of the field, which is here today and tomorrow is thrown into the fire, will he not much more clothe you, O you of little faith? So do not worry, saying, 'What shall we drink?' or 'What shall we eat?' or 'What shall we wear?' For the pagans run after all

Personal Notes

these things, and your heavenly Father knows that you need them. But seek first his kingdom and his righteousness, and all these things will be given to you as well. Therefore do not worry about tomorrow, for tomorrow will worry about itself. Each day has enough trouble of its own."

Matthew 6:24–34

Further Insight

In his book *The American Idea of Success,* Richard Huber wrote: "In America, success has meant making money and translating it into status, or becoming famous. . . . It was not the same thing as happiness—which is how you feel. It recorded a change in rank, the upgrading of a person in relation to others by the unequal distribution of money and power, prestige and fame. . . . Success was not simply being rich or famous. It means attaining riches or achieving fame. You had to know where a man began and where he ended in order to determine how far he had come."

In America, success means making it in terms of money, power and fame. And as the Swedish sociologist Gunnar Myrdal is reported to have said, "Americans worship success." So the cross of Jesus may be a less accurate symbol of what we in fact worship than, say, a solid gold Cadillac—or in today's energy crisis, a solid gold Volkswagen!

There are no unchanging road maps. Couples are searching in fear and hope to find their own way to live their needs, wants, thoughts and loves. Henry Miller comments, "Love in marriage must be a constant recreation of that which caused it to

Comments

happen in the first place, namely, expanding one's mind, ungreediness, self-knowledge, a little of the public be damned, a willingness for tears, a sense of ending."

From Raines,
Success Is a Moving Target, pp. 13–14, 18–19.

Questions to Discuss

1. Realistically speaking, money to us is . . .

2. When I think of God and money and our marriage, I feel . . .

3. The ways I would like us to change our thinking about money are . . .

Our Prayer

O God, as we struggle with money and its place in our lives, help us not to be so foolish as to feel that it is unimportant, nor to be so deluded as to feel that it is all-important. . . .

Amen.

27

The Practical Approach to Financial Needs

"It was as if I had thrown a live hand grenade . . ."

PAUL:

Sybil and I affectionately called him "The Czar." He literally had been a member of the Board of Trustees and the Board of Deacons for fifty years and chairman of the latter for twenty. He sometimes had single-handedly held that little church together so that its witness for Christ could go forward. Because of his great faithfulness, virtually nothing was done in the church without this man's approval.

For years this church had been pastored by a student from the seminary; for years they had paid a very small salary. In fact, when Sybil and I moved there, my first year's salary was $1,800 plus a parsonage. Sybil taught school while I was in seminary, but we gave our souls to that church. Because the community around us was growing, the church also grew.

Finally it came time for the discussion of the pastor's salary at the finance-committee meeting preparing the annual budget. Thinking I was acting in a very humble, Christian way, I excused myself so they could decide on my salary for the coming year. Because we had given ourselves so much to the church and because it was doing so well, we were confident that the finance committee would respond appropriately. I didn't see that section of the budget until a week later, when it was presented at the church business meeting, but I was disappointed. They proposed only a $200 increase in salary for me for the next year! Because Sybil had her teacher's salary, we were able to survive. For the next year

133

we gave ourselves to the work of Christ in that church, and the community continued to respond enthusiastically to the church.

Once again it was time for the annual finance-committee meeting. Sybil and I had talked and decided we wanted to begin our family as soon as we could, which meant she would not be teaching school any longer. We evaluated our family budget. We studied the current strong financial picture of the church and looked at its promising future. It was then that we decided to ask for an annual salary of $3,600, expecting them to make a counter offer with which we could "negotiate."

The finance-committee meeting began. We discussed the other aspects of the budget and then it came time to consider the pastor's salary. Instead of excusing myself, I remained and told them that Sybil and I planned to begin our family, that she would no longer be teaching school, and that I needed a salary of $3,600. That was a hundred-percent increase in less than two years! It was as if I had thrown a live hand grenade into the committee meeting and everyone was waiting for it to explode! For thirty seconds there was total silence and then "The Czar" spoke very quietly and said, "I think we should give the pastor the salary he's asked for. That's what this church needs, to learn responsibility and challenge." The committee unanimously approved the motion. It was presented to the church a week later, and the recommendation of the finance committee was accepted.

I learned a couple of important lessons that day, one of which was that the church did respect a financial need that was clearly and logically presented. Another lesson was that every pastor needs to stand up for himself and for his own practical concerns. A congregation, as loving as it might be, may not automatically know all of the pastor's needs. It is important that we focus on those needs and call them to the attention of the appropriate board or committee so that the congregation can have the opportunity of responding with love and responsibility, which they usually do.

Scripture   **Personal Notes**

The elders who direct the affairs of the church well are worthy of double honor, especially those whose work is preaching and teaching. For the Scripture says, "Do not muzzle the ox while it is treading out the grain," and "The worker deserves his wages."
1 Timothy 5:17–18

Further Insight   **Comments**

There is a close connection between family financial planning, economics, and the New Testament concept of stewardship. That connection is "oikonomia," the Greek root of our English word, "economics."

Modern economics has become a science that studies the many factors affecting the production, distribution, and use of the world's resources. Yet in the first century, oikonomia referred simply to the ordinary management decisions made in every household. It applied especially to persons who had responsibility for managing the property of another. In the translation of this New Testament term into English, oikonomia became "stewardship."

The starting place of stewardship is in family economics. The two belong together.

In the parables of Jesus, stewards are held accountable for the use they make of the resources entrusted to their care. Jesus was clearly looking for stewards who would be faithful and prudent in household management and the management of all resources.

From National Council of Churches,
Christians Doing Financial Planning.

Questions to Discuss

1. I think our salary from the church is . . .

2. As a couple, I think we manage our money . . .

3. I would like to improve the management of our income by . . .

Our Prayer

O God, help us to manage our lives and our money in such a way that they both will glorify you and bless our lives individually and together as a couple. . . .

Amen.

28

Fun and Laughter

"I sure wish God would make somebody cheerful around this place!"

SYBIL:

It was a difficult time in our family. I was recuperating at home following a week in the hospital for a compressed vertebra. Paul's mother was staying with us to care for me, run the household, oversee four children, and manage Cleopatra, our unruly pet English bulldog. Paul was feeling especially pressured by congregational needs and the additional family demands. The children were experiencing the stress of Mom's illness and the upset in our family routine. I was finding the restrictions and incapacitation of my injury extremely frustrating. In general, there was tension for everyone. A mood of depression pervaded our household as we sat around the kitchen table to eat dinner one evening. Paul's mother reported that "Cleo" had given her a particularly difficult time that day, running away in the snow when she opened the door to receive a mail delivery. Paul and I corrected one of the children's table manners and stifled a quarrelsome exchange between two others. All of us ate in strained silence for a few minutes, lost in our own thoughts. An air of tension prevailed in the kitchen until our five-year-old broke the mood with a wistful "I sure wish God would make somebody cheerful around this place!"

That one brief comment made us realize how intense we had been. We laughed, relaxed, and began chatting in a lighter way with each other. The food even tasted better.

A basic ingredient in any marriage and family is the positive approach brought into the relationship. An attitude of joy can turn the dullest, most routine experiences into times of fun.

137

A good-humored disposition also requires that we allow time in our schedules for fun activities. Ball games, neighborhood parties, sitting quietly in front of the fireplace, going to a movie, walking in the moonlight, taking a vacation together—all of this means scheduling time for those extra events. For years, Monday has been Paul's day off, and Monday night has been family night at our house. We play games, make popcorn, enjoy a fire when it is cold, and spend the evening together at home. And these fun events do not have to cost money. Taking a walk in the park, lying on a beach, building a snowman, talking together about a book we both have read—none of these costs a cent.

Along with this, however, sometimes money can and should be budgeted for special events. A vacation, a surprise dinner at a fine restaurant, or even a hamburger at a fast-food place does take money, but it can be planned into the total family budget. When our children were young, vacations were usually inexpensive trips to visit relatives and grandparents. Paul and I also took several brief vacations by ourselves during this time and squeezed them out of our limited finances. We learned that time and money can somehow be arranged if our priorities include fun in our lives.

For a marriage to grow and be fulfilling, laughter, fun, and joy must be part of it. The joy we experience together is the result not only of moving spiritual experiences, but also of the exhilaration of sex, the pleasures of close friendships or of deep sharing in the family, and the rewards of personal growth. Joy and laughter provide an important foundation stone for a minister's marriage.

Scripture

A happy heart makes the face cheerful, but heartache crushes the spirit.

The discerning heart seeks knowledge, but the mouth of a fool feeds on folly.

All the days of the oppressed are wretched, but the cheerful heart has a continual feast.

Proverbs 15:13–15

Personal Notes

Further Insight

Dr. Hitig said it was clear to him that there was nothing undersized about my will to live. He said that

Comments

what was more important was that I continue to believe in everything I had said. He shared my excitement about the possibilities of recovery and liked the idea of a partnership.

Even before we had completed arrangements for moving out of the hospital we began the part of the program calling for the full exercise of the affirmative emotions as a factor in enhancing body chemistry. It was easy enough to hope and love and have faith, but what about laughter? Nothing is less funny than being flat on your back with all the bones in your spine and joints hurting. A systematic program was indicated. A good place to begin, I thought, was with amusing movies. Allen Funt, producer of the spoofing television program *Candid Camera,* sent films of some of his *CC* classics along with a motion-picture projector. The nurse was instructed in its use.

It worked. I made the joyous discovery that ten minutes of genuine belly laughter had an anesthetic effect and would give me at least two hours of pain-free sleep. When the pain-killing effect of the laughter wore off, we would switch on the motion-picture projector again, and, not infrequently, it would lead to another pain-free sleep interval. Sometimes, the nurse read to me out of a trove of humor books. Especially useful were J. B. and Katherine White's *Subtreasury of American Humor* and Max Eastman's *The Enjoyment of Laughter.*

How scientific was it to believe that laughter—as well as the positive emotions in general—was affecting my body chemistry for the better? If laughter did in fact have a salutary

effect on the body's chemistry, it
seemed at least theoretically likely that
it would enhance the system's ability
to fight the inflammation. So we took
sedimentation-rate readings just before
as well as several hours after the
laughter episodes. Each time, there
was a drop of at least five points. The
drop by itself was not substantial, but
it held and was cumulative. I was
greatly elated by the discovery that
there is a physiologic basis for the
ancient theory that laughter is good
medicine.

From Cousins, "Anatomy of an Illness
(As Perceived by the Patient)," pp. 39–40.

Questions to Discuss

1. In the past, the events that have brought me great joy are . . .

2. I think the time we spend on laughing and having fun together is
   . . .

3. I would like to add more joy, fun, and laughter to our lives by . . .

Our Prayer

O God, help us to be so open to you, to ourselves, and to each other, that
we might see and feel the deep joy that floods life all around us. . . .

Amen.

29

The Spiritual Life in Christian Marriage

"I just can't believe it!"

PAUL:

There is a practice that has meant much to Sybil and me all the years of our marriage. It has become such a part of our life together that we don't even realize we are doing it.

We were in Athens on our first trip to Europe in 1980. We had been staying in a small Greek hotel for four or five days, and every morning we had gone downstairs for the continental breakfast. During our married years, our practice has been that before every meal we hold hands, quietly bow our heads, share a short blessing for the food, and then share a kiss. For over twenty-five years we have done that, and we do it whether we are in the privacy of our own home, in the most elegant restaurant, or, as then, in a small Greek hotel.

Everyone in Europe had been warm and friendly to us, except for this one particular hotel manager. I don't know whether it was because his English was limited and our contemporary Greek was absolutely nil, whether he was just an angry person, or if there was something maladjusted in his personal life. Whatever it was, he was probably the most unfriendly person we met on our trip. On the last day we were there, I paid our bill and picked up our suitcases. As we headed for the door, the hotel manager called, "Hey, come back here." My first thought was that he was going to try to tack another expense onto our bill. Instead, when we went back to his desk, he looked me in the eye and said, "Every morning when you and your wife came down to breakfast, you joined hands, bowed your heads, mumbled some words, and then blew a kiss to each other across the table. What were you doing?" I responded, "We're

Christians and we believe that God loves every human being—that God loves us and God loves you. So we were thanking God for his love for us. We were thanking God for your beautiful country and for the safety of your hotel, and we were asking God to bless our family." He looked at me for a minute, scratched his head, and then said with his heavy accent, "I just can't believe it! I just can't believe it!"

The real point is that we did not even realize we were doing this. It had become as natural to share in that time of spiritual fellowship as to put on our shoes in the morning before going outside.

A strong spiritual emphasis has always been at the heart of our relationship and our marital commitment. Our courtship began as we were prayer partners together. Praying for each other and reading the Scriptures every day kept our hearts together for the three years of our separation during our engagement.

After we married, holding hands, praying, and sharing a kiss became a part of every meal. When we get ready for bed, from the very beginning of our marriage we have read a portion of Scripture or a devotion from a devotional book and then shared in prayer. It is at this time that we pray for members of our church, pray for world issues, pray for our children, pray for ourselves and any special problems we might be confronting. It is this special time that has allowed us also to discuss many intricacies of our relationship in the context of a spiritual atmosphere.

A further experience has been an evening devotional for our whole family at the dinner table. Here, we read a story from a Bible-story book, discuss it in a very simple way, and then share in conversational prayer—a special experience that allows every person to participate. These spiritual experiences have enriched our relationships and family life tremendously. The strength of the spiritual aspect of marriage is that it empowers us when we are weak, promotes forgiveness when we have fallen, and focuses our attention on a Creator God to thank for our blessings.

Scripture	Personal Notes

I will extol the LORD at all
    times;
his praise will always be on my
    lips.
My soul will boast in the LORD;
   let the afflicted hear and
    rejoice.
Glorify the LORD with me;
   let us exalt his name
    together.

I sought the LORD, and he
      answered me;
   he delivered me from all my
      fears.
Those who look to him are radi-
      ant;
   their faces are never covered
      with shame.
This poor man called, and the
      LORD heard him;
   he saved him out of all his
      troubles.
The angel of the LORD encamps
      around those who fear
         him,
   and he delivers them.
Taste and see that the LORD is
      good;
   blessed is the man who takes
      refuge in him.
Fear the LORD, you his saints,
   for those who fear him lack
      nothing.
                              Psalm 34:1–9

Further Insight   **Comments**

Intimacy is the interlocking of two
individual persons joined by a bond
which partially overcomes their sepa-
rateness. In the fullest expression of
intimacy there is a vertical dimension,
a sense of relatedness to the universe
which both strengthens the marital
relationship and is strengthened by
it. Quite apart from any churchy or
churchly considerations, the spiritual
dimension of marriage is a practical
source of food for marital growth and
health. No single factor does more to
give a marriage joy or to keep it both
a venture and an adventure in mutual
fulfillment than shared commitment
to spiritual discovery. The life of
the spirit is deeply personal, so that

moments of sharing on the spiritual
level are tender, precious moments in
a relationship.

By spiritual intimacy is meant the
sense of a vital relationship with that
which transcends our brief, fragile
existence—a relationship with the
calm of values and meanings, with the
flow of history and life about us, and
with that "ultimate concern" (Tillich)
which we call God. The need for a
sense of spiritual intimacy includes
the need for a sense of "at-homeness"
in the universe, and a deeply experienced feeling of what Erik Erikson
calls "basic trust." The need for this
kind of intimacy is a fundamental one,
both for the individual and for his
marriage. St. Augustine's well-known
words, "Thou has made us for Thyself
and our hearts are restless till they rest
in Thee," emphasize the fact that the
will to relate to the Spirit of life is an
inescapable part of man's hunger for
depth relationships.

From Clinebell and Clinebell,
The Intimate Marriage, pp. 179–80.

Questions to Discuss

1. I believe our spiritual intimacy has been . . .

2. For me, some of our most important times of spiritual sharing have been . . .

3. I would like to improve our spiritual life together by . . .

Our Prayer

O God, help us to magnify you and exalt your name together. May the strength of our mutual spiritual life bond our lives as a couple. . . .

Amen.

30

Communicating Spiritual Values

"Daddy, are we flying upside down?"

SYBIL:

When our second daughter was just two years old, she, her sister, Paul, and I were flying back to the East Coast from the Midwest, where we had visited relatives. As she sat on Paul's lap and looked out the window of the airplane, our tiny toddler turned to him and asked, "Daddy, are we flying upside down?" He responded, "No, honey. Why do you ask?" To which she replied as she pointed below the plane, "Well, the clouds are down there." We were amazed at that comment from a two-year-old.

We have been continually amazed at the way children grasp the values and priorities of our lives in an upside-down world. For example, a few years ago we were figuring our income taxes and for hours had gone through our checkbooks, bills, statements and records until, finally, we had categorized all our expenses. That year we had three children in college, one of whom had been in a university overseas. We knew the expenses had been heavy, but had not realized they had been as great as the computed figures revealed. In consternation Paul lamented, "Do you realize that last year the money we spent for education and for our giving to the church amounted to almost half of my salary?"

Our youngest daughter, a high-school sophomore at the time, was in the next room working on an assignment for school. Instantly she came into the room where we were and commented, "I'm proud to be part of a family whose top priorities are education and God's work." We hadn't thought about it in those terms and were grateful both for her insight and her sharing it with us. Her comment altered our perspective. Spiritual

values do influence the decisions and choices we make, even uncon-
sciously, and they do get communicated to our children.

| Scripture | Personal Notes |

Scripture

May the God who gives endurance
and encouragement give you a spirit
of unity among yourselves as you follow Christ Jesus, so that with one
heart and mouth you may glorify the
God and Father of our Lord Jesus
Christ.

Accept one another, then, just as
Christ accepted you, in order to bring
praise to God. For I tell you that
Christ has become a servant of the
Jews on behalf of God's truth, to con-
firm the promises made to the patri-
archs so that the Gentiles may glorify
God for his mercy, as it is written:

"Therefore I will praise you
    among the Gentiles;
  I will sing hymns to your
    name."

Again, it says,
  "Rejoice, O Gentiles, with
    his people."

And again,
  "Praise the Lord, all you
    Gentiles,
  and sing praises to him, all
    you peoples."

And again, Isaiah says,
  "The root of Jesse will spring
    up,
  one who will arise to rule
    over the nations;
  the Gentiles will hope in
    him."

May the God of hope fill you with
all joy and peace as you trust in him,
so that you may overflow with hope
by the power of the Holy Spirit.

Romans 15:5–13

Further Insight

The possibilities for marital cre-
ativity are almost limitless: sharing in
helping to create a much needed
community service, a new approach to
civil rights, a more humane approach
to divorce laws, a new park, a group
for intellectual enjoyment and serious
study, a better mousetrap, a plan for
increasing person-to-person relating
across ethnic, racial and national
boundaries, a program for helping eli-
gible young adults to meet potential
marriage partners; a new way of
approaching disciplining one's children, celebrating holidays, taking
trips, getting the household chores
done efficiently, enjoying sex, participating in church, creating opportunities for fun in the family, and so on ad
infinitum. "And without creation, love
is an abstraction—a mere puff of wind
. . . a gust of emotion."

MacIver, at the close of his book,
poses the question of the ages—a
question which every married couple
should raise together: What makes life
worthwhile? . . .

One of the mysteries and marvels
of intimacy in marriage is that it offers
so many opportunities to find those
shared transcendent meanings that
ultimately make life worthwhile.

From Clinebell and Clinebell,
The Intimate Marriage, pp. 197–98.

Comments

Questions to Discuss

(First take out your checkbook and date book and review the last three
    months.)

1. According to our checkbooks and personal calendars, our top
    priorities were . . .

2. I would like the top priorities of our marriage to be . . .

3. To initiate those priorities, I think we need to . . .

Our Prayer

O God, help us to love you with all of our heart, mind, soul, and strength.
May every segment of our lives reflect those priority choices. . . .

Amen.

Epilogue: The Continuing Saga

"Hey, we're poppin' a wheelie!"

PAUL:

It happened when we were visiting our favorite island in the Aegean Sea, a hundred miles from Athens. We had rented a motor scooter to go around the island and visit the various sights, as we had done several times in Rome and Athens. Since I had a Moped at home, a motor scooter was nothing new or threatening to either of us.

But I had not previously ridden this particular Italian motor scooter, which had a hand clutch and hand-controlled manual transmission. When I took it out on the road to get used to it before Sybil joined me, I noticed that the scooter had a lot of power, and the clutch was so tight that it had a hair-trigger tension to it. One moment it would be in neutral, but a millimeter of a release of the clutch brought it to full power almost instantly.

SYBIL:

I climbed on behind Paul, and we decided to go to a hotel to say farewell to some new friends who were leaving for their home in England. As we traveled down the road toward the hotel, all was right in our world. We were on a beautiful sunny island and were totally enjoying life, each other, and our vacation. We were trapped behind a slow-moving car when we caught sight of the entrance to the hotel. Since the driveway leading up to the hotel was quite steep and we were moving slowly, it was necessary to shift into low and accelerate very quickly to make it up the approach to the hotel.

We hit the incline, Paul shifted down, accelerated to full power, and let out the trigger clutch. But he had not taken into account one very important factor. With me on the bike behind him, the center of gravity had shifted slightly to the rear—and that's when disaster happened.

151

PAUL:

As I felt the front wheel begin to come off the ground, I turned to look at Sybil and laughingly said, "Hcy, we're poppin' a wheelie!" But it didn't stop there—before I could get my head turned back to face the front, the full throttle, the hair-trigger clutch, the shifted center of gravity, and the steep incline all conspired against us and the "wheelie" never stopped. We were suddenly in a ridiculous yet frightening position. Sybil was flat on her back on the street, and I was on my back on top of her, while I desperately tried to hold the fully throttled roaring monster of a motor scooter off both of us with my hands, arms, legs, and feet.

A Greek woman and two passing tourists rushed to our rescue and helped to lift off the scooter. Miraculously, we survived—with only a skinned elbow for Sybil and nothing more than a wounded ego for me. We took Sybil back to our hotel to tend her wound. She rested for a few minutes while I went out to tame the motor scooter. Within a half hour, we were on the road again, heading back to visit our friends and spend an exciting day exploring the island.

PAUL and SYBIL:

Many marriages are a lot like that ride. They start out with excitement, laughter, joy, togetherness and then—because the center of gravity has shifted or there is more power present than they expected—an accident happens and a choice presents itself. Do you scuttle the whole experience? Do you push and pull that accident around for the rest of your lives? Or do you get back on the motor scooter of marriage, having learned from the mistake, and enjoy the thrill of the ride together again?

We have chosen to learn from the accidents in our marriage. So we have committed ourselves to continue building a growing, intimate relationship. We invite you to join us.

Our Own Evaluation

After 30 days with the work/play book, our marriage . . .

The chapters and categories that were most helpful to us were . . .

It would have been helpful to us if you had included the issue of . . .

Additional suggestions are . . .

Name _____

Address _____

_____

_____

We'd welcome your reactions to this book, Please send them to

Paul and Sybil Eppinger
7000 North Central Ave.
Phoenix AZ 85020